# LELAND

# &

# FERN BOLT

*Heritage, Family, Business and City Service*

## Leland Emet Bolt

authorHOUSE®

*AuthorHouse™*
*1663 Liberty Drive*
*Bloomington, IN 47403*
*www.authorhouse.com*
*Phone: 1 (800) 839-8640*

*Published by AuthorHouse  02/22/2018*

*ISBN: 978-1-5462-1254-6 (sc)*
*ISBN: 978-1-5462-1252-2 (hc)*
*ISBN: 978-1-5462-1253-9 (e)*

*Library of Congress Control Number: 2017915621*

*Print information available on the last page.*

# PREFACE

I was born in 1928 at Payette Idaho, and grew up in nearby Emmett. We were close to my Brubaker grandparents, Emet Hill Brubaker and Myrtie Edna (Fulton) Brubaker, and mother's sister, Iris Eliza (Brubaker) Mordhorst and her husband Edward Mordhorst. The families were close, and took turns hosting celebrations, like Easter, Thanksgiving, Christmas, and the New Year.

When still an infant, mom took me to visit my Bolt Grandparents, Benjamin Darius Bolt and Lotta Elbourne (Zimmerman) Bolt, about 200 miles away on their fruit farm near Freewater, Oregon. When I was older, mom and dad took me to the farm each year, for a month or two with the grandparents. When a teenager, grandpa Bolt showed me a loose-leaf book of typed (by Aunt Martha) pages that he titled "To My Children". These were never published working papers, but after he died the pages were reproduced for each of his 4 children.

Years later, I found dad's copy of "To My Children", and began to build the genealogical dates, events and stories of our relatives. The people, events and records and associated sources are entered in my Family Tree Maker (FTM) genealogy computer program. With years of research, my data base grew to over 5,000 persons, including dates, places and sources. Every year the FTM is updated for new ancestors or information about them.

I wanted this book to be the story of the people, conditions they faced and how they met their challenges. It is about the family of my parents, Leland Eddy Bolt and Fern Leoline (Brubaker) Bolt. Their story is preceded by Leland and Fern's grandparents and parents, then my parents' lives and accomplishments. The Appendix shows some of their genealogical "roots" – at least what can be reliably proven.

Many family members have contributed to this book, as will be seen in the references and bibliography. Also, I must acknowledge the help and comments of others in the review process. Drew Rogers worked with his grandmother (Martha) and others on Van Donge family details. Joan (Clemmons) Bolt provided lots of detail developed by my Cousin, Benjamin Hamele Bolt (deceased), on the Benjamin Draper Bolt family. Cousins, Ann (Denman) Hultgren and Carol (Denman) Holst provided details about the Kenneth Denman & Margaret (Bolt) Denman Family. Cousins Mary (Collier) Buck and her brother, Michael Collier, helped with information on the Charles Collier and Hazel (Brubaker) Collier family. Cousin Melanie (Mordhorst) Entzminger helped with Edward Mordhorst & Iris (Brubaker) Mordhorst families. Robert Van Donge and his sisters, Carolee (Van Donge) White and Connie (Van Donge) Rogers, provided details of the lives of their Van Donge parents.

ID: 759480

# CHAPTER 1
## The Bolt Grandparents

# SECTION 1

# The Families of Charles Bolt

CHARLES BOLT was born in Highland County, Ohio, December 30, 1831. In 1851 his parents, John and Karenhappuch (Horton) Bolt, moved to Hamilton County, Indiana. When a teenager, he was apprenticed to learn the brick masonry trade. In 1855 the family moved to Montgomery County, Iowa. On the trip, Charles shot a deer, the antlers of which hung for many years in his son, Benjamin's, front hall. The family settled in the tiny farming community of Frankfort, Iowa, where they bought farm lands. Charles' educational opportunities were meager, but he made the most of them. He worked as a bricklayer and then engaged in general contracting.

In December 1857, 26 year-old Charles Bolt got the County contract for a bridge over the "Big Tarkie" on the County road east of Frankfort, which was the County seat. Prominent families in the Frankfort area were; the Bonds, Hortons and Straits. Dr. Amasa Bond and the Hortons were close relatives of Charles Bolt, and the Straits were a merchant family. Charles courted seventeen year-old Miss Alzina J. Strait, and they married 4 March 1858. Charles bought a farm nearby and built their home. Their daughter, Lillian Alzina Bolt, was born 15 January 1859. That year, tragedy struck when her mother was burned to death. Her clothes ignited from a wood stove. Charles and his motherless daughter returned to live with his parents on their Frankfort farm.

In 1860, Joseph M. Hewitt and his family were living at the Frankfort Central House, which they owned and operated. Charles Bolt was then constructing a County bridge across the Nishnabotna river. Between work periods Charles Bolt found time to court Joseph M. Hewitt's daughter, Margaret. Charles and Margaret Ann Hewitt married 3 July

1860. Charles' uncle, County Judge James Riley Horton, performed the ceremony. It was the first marriage in the town of Red Oak. The couple are in Pictures (101) and (102).

*Charles Bolt, the Mason.*

*Margaret Ann Hewitt.*

In 1860 the clouds of the Civil War were forming, and reached into Iowa. Charles continued his masonry contracting business, and their first child, Etta Vilura, was born in Red Oak 19 January 1862.

On 13 March 1863 the Iowa Governor appointed Charles a 1st LT in the Iowa State Militia. He carried an 1851 36-Cal percussion cap & ball side arm. This Colt Revolving Pistol was Colt's first practical revolver. The well-balanced Navy model packed an impressive punch, and was a favorite of such diverse pistoleros as "Wild Bill" Hickok and Frank James. This model [shown in Picture (103)] also played a major role in the post-war western expansion and saw use well into the cartridge era.

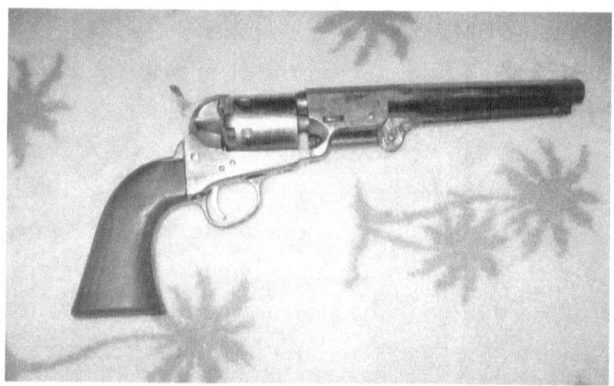

*Charles Bolt's Navy Model 36 Caliber Pistol.*

As Montgomery County Sherriff and a 1ˢᵗ Lt in the Iowa Militia, Charles made dangerous trips across the prairie, taking deserters and "copperheads" (active Confederate sympathizers) to Des Moines. When he made these trips, Margaret Ann was left alone with the children. She was frightened, as "sympathizers" had threatened to burn their house down. One night while she was alone with the children, she heard someone trying to get in a window. She kept an axe by the bed, and so arming herself stood by the window with the axe raised. A man raised the window, but before entering, turned and spit. She put the axe down for she recognized the gesture. Charles Bolt chewed tobacco. She thereafter said that, while she never liked his habit of chewing tobacco, at least it saved his life on one occasion.

In 1864 the Bolts sold the house in town and bought a farm just beyond the Hewitt farm south of Red Oak. In 1864 and 1865 Charles was deputy provost marshal of Montgomery and Adams counties. He was also a partner in Bolt & Hendrix, contractors and builders. He built the majority of the brick buildings of Red Oak; and the firm also did a large business in adjoining counties.

Frankfort was the county seat until 1865 when it was relocated to Red Oak. That year Charles Bolt contracted all the brickwork on the second school building in Red Oak. W. H. Kerrihard was the general contractor and the district could not pay, so Kerrihard retained control of it. It was used as a school, a church, and a dance hall until the district raised the money.

A son, Henry Albert Bolt, was born October 28th, 1865, to Charles and Margaret Bolt in their new house on the farm near the Hewitts. In 1866 there was considerable controversy over the location of the Montgomery County Courthouse. The county decided to move the Courthouse, a two story frame structure 18 feet by 36 feet, from Frankfort to Red Oak. Red Oak agreed pay for the moving. Histories state Wayne Stennett was given the contract and the building was put on huge sleds to await the first snow. Snows came in December. So Wayne Stennett and his party harnessed thirty yoke of oxen to draw the huge sleds and the building thereon. They moved slowly northward around the dividing ridge between the waters of the creeks. After turning westward in a blizzard, they were off course after some miles. They unhitched the oxen and went home. The court house was lost on the prairie for some days.

A family version is that while the discussions of when, how and if were going on, some young fellows decided to settle the matter by "stealing" the old court house and moving it to Red Oak. Charles Bolt was said to be the leader and James Horton, a sixteen year old cousin, was in the party. Waiting for a heavy snowfall, they put the building on logs and carted it away by ox teams. But they did not anticipate the severe blizzard. In the darkness of night and with the storm raging, they lost their direction and had to abandon the building several miles off course. The court house was lost, and was not found for some time. The young men preferred to conceal their identity and it remained sort of "hush, hush". Wayne Stennett, who found the building, contracted the moving project for its eventual arrival in Red Oak. It was fixed up and served for many years.

The year after the Courthouse move, Charles Bolt was elected to the Board of Supervisors. He was then thirty-six years of age.

Charles and Margaret's second son, Benjamin Darius Bolt, was born March 28th, 1868 in the house on the farm.

In 1870 Charles Bolt was elected Master of the local Masonic Lodge, of which he was a charter member. That year he started construction of the East Ward or Lincoln school as general contractor. He was a man of great natural ability, as well as unusual physical strength. Because of a lack of technical training he had acquired his own methods of finding areas of circles, cylindrical contents, etc., all of which were workable and remarkably accurate. During the building of the Lincoln school building in Red Oak in 1870, it was necessary to place a stone (keystone) in position over the entrance. Two of his men were unable to handle it, so he took the stone on his shoulders and carried it up the ladder and placed it in the position, where it still stands.

Charles, working as a partner first in Bolt Crockett & Company, and later Bolt Hendrix & Company, built most of the early buildings in Red Oak (e.g. Lincoln, Washington and Jefferson schools; the County Jail and the Methodist Church), and in neighboring towns of Malvern, Glenwood, and Clarinda. He also built the County Court houses at Cherokee and Gundy Center, Iowa, and in Nelson and Freemont, Nebraska.

Margaret Ann Hewitt was the head of the family much of the time, while Charles was building in other towns and away on his duties as Marshall or as an officer in the Iowa Militia during the Civil war. She wrote poetry and was closely involved in the children's education.

Charles and Margaret were members of the Methodist Episcopal Church, and the parents of six children:

- Etta Vilura, born 19 January 1862 and died 3 March 1890. See Picture (104).

*Etta Vilura Bolt.*

- Henry Albert, born 18 October 1865 and died 27 October 1911. See Picture (105).

*Henry Albert Bolt.*

- **Benjamin Darius, born 28 March 1868 and died 1 January 1956** See Picture (106).

*Benjamin Darius Bolt.*

- Maude Arlina, born 8 December 1871 and died 24 May 1958. See Picture (107).

*Maude Arlina Bolt*

- Myrtle Adelia, born 21 February 1877 and died 19 January 1966. See Picture (108).

*Myrtle Adelia Bolt*

- Nina Leona, born 15 October 1879 and died? See Picture (109)

*Nina Leona Bolt*

# References:

1. Martin, Nina Leona, & Bolt, Ronald Ben, Bolt Americana; Copyright Reserved 1968; Published by Ronald Ben Bolt 25840 Bunker Hill Blvd. Hayward, California 94542
2. Horton, A. J., The Descendants of Adam Rector; Published by Carl J. Ward Printing, Buffalo, NY, 1915
3. Obituary, Margaret Ann (Hewitt) Bolt Red Oak Express Newspaper 22 April 1932
4. Obituary, Charles Bolt, Red Oak Express Newspaper 26 April 1912

# SECTION 2

# The Chauncey Zimmerman and Jerusha Adelle Eddy Family

Chauncey W. Zimmerman obtained a common school education and learned the carpenter trade of Nicholas Rector and Albert Flint, commencing at the age of 17. He married 25 February 1873 Jerusha Adelle Eddy, daughter of Samuel Eddy and Harriet C. Nichols. She was born 10 August 1853

After marriage, Chauncey purchased a farm near Evans, New York. He remained there 12 years, then moved the family to Springville, NY, and engaged in carpenter work for 10 years. He took a drawing course with a Chicago engineer, and then worked in the carpentry and millwright professions. He made an art of his occupation, and detested the cheap and shoddy. The life he lived was clean, simple, and industrious. For many years he was a member of the Independent Order of Odd Fellows (IOOF), and subscribed to the faith of the Baptist Church. Chauncey is shown in Picture (110).

*Chauncey W. Zimmerman*

Their children were: **Lotta Elbourne, Born 8 October 1874 at North Boston, NY.** See Picture (111); Mattie A., born 23 December 1875 at North Boston, NY. See Picture (112), and Eddy C. Zimmerman, born 26 June 1880 at Evans, NY. See Picture (113).

*Lotta Elbourne Zimmerman*

*Mattie A. Zimmerman*

*Eddy C. Zimmerman*

Lotta Elbourne Zimmerman graduated from Griffith Institute of Buffalo, NY, with a teaching credential. She became a teacher in Red Oak, Iowa, schools. There she met and married Benjamin Darius Bolt. See Chapter 2, section 1 for their lives and family.

Mattie A. Zimmerman married Ottamar Hamele (b. 19 April 1878). Ottamar is shown in Picture (114). The marriage was conducted by phone 27 June 1904, recorded in East Otto, New York. Ottamar learned his father's harness-making trade, then worked on a farm three years. In 1894, he and his older brother, Otto, started the East Otto Advance. They managed that newspaper together until 1899, when Ottamar began law studies at the office of E. A. Scott, Springville, New York. He passed the examinations and graduated in 1900 from Springville's Griffith Institute in Buffalo, New York, without having attended the school. After three years of law school, Ottamar entered into a partnership with the E. A. Scott law firm, serving until 1912. He and his wife then went to Pawhuska, Oklahoma, where he had a law practice. He was assistant Osage County Prosecuting Attorney in 1913 and 1914. In the 1930s Ottamar was a Federal Counsel in the Franklin D. Roosevelt administration. Though Mattie died 3 September 1936, Ottamar continued to be a great help for the family of his brother-in-law, Benjamin Darius Bolt. He helped their son, Benjamin Draper Bolt get training and become an FBI agent in Washington, D. C. He also helped their daughter, Martha, get Government sponsored nurse's training and introduced her to Washington D. C. society.

*Ottamar Hamele.*

Little is known about Eddy C. Zimmerman. He left their western New York area and the family lost track of him.

Jerusha (Eddy) Zimmerman died 26 June 1911. Chauncey married Jennie Sisler 6 September 1913. She was born 6 August 1867. Chauncey died 6 June 1929 in Washington, D. C., at the home of his daughter, Mattie, and her husband, Ottamar Hamele.

## References:

1. Horton, A. J., The Descendents of Adam Rector, Carl J. Ward Printing, Buffalo, NY, 1915, pg 12).
2. C. W. Zimmerman Obituary, Springville, NY, Journal, 13 Jun 1929.
3. Bolt, Benjamin Darius, To My Children, an unpublished manuscript provided to each of his children in 1957.

# SECTION 3

# The Family of Alvah Humbert
# Brubaker & Anna Marie Hill

Alvah Humbert, "A. H.", Brubaker was born to Abraham Brubaker and his wife, Martha Ann Parker, Oct. 16, 1846, on a farm near Logansport, Indiana - one of their 12 children. Abraham was a carpenter, who taught his seven sons his trade and farming. A. H. farmed with his father in Indiana and Eldena, Illinois, until 1868, when he married Anna Marie Hill at Dixon, Ill, little knowing at the time, the couple was to live together as man and wife for 73 years. He remembered that when a small boy he met Abraham Lincoln at a debate in rural Illinois. Perhaps that explains why he was such a strong Republican. At the debate, he said Douglas accused Abe Lincoln of running a saloon. Lincoln's retort to the accusation was that he didn't deny running the saloon, but said "Little Stephen was his best customer".

After marriage, the Brubakers farmed in Iowa, Illinois and Nebraska. A. H. entered the general mercantile business in 1888. In 1893 he established his own general mercantile business in Oketo, Kansas, which he operated until 1905. Besides raising a large family, Anna Marie (Hill) Brubaker established a millinery shop in Oketo. A. H. was Marshall County (Kansas) Treasurer several times. He purchased the Bigelow State Bank and moved to Bigelow, Kansas, where he was Bank President and Cashier for 10 years. His daughter, Lulu, helped run the Bank. About 4:00 PM Thursday evening, 24 December 1910, A. H. and Lulu foiled a bank robbery. The robber waited until all patrons had left, then pulled his gun and demanded the money. At one point he began hitting A. H. on the head with his gun. Lulu pulled her gun from the drawer and shot him. She shot him again as he exited the door. She was awarded a gold watch for her bravery. A. H. later sold the bank to his son, Harlowe, and moved first to Morenci, Arizona, then in 1924 to Payette, Idaho. Upon reaching his 100$^{th}$ birthday he was made Honorary Mayor of Payette on each birthday. A fiercely loyal Republican, he walked to town each day and the locals enjoyed stirring his political anger. He was highly regarded by both family and residents of Payette. He took a keen interest in community affairs and politics, and never failed to vote!

A. H. and Anna's children were:

- Blanche, who died in infancy
- Nathan Abraham Brubaker, born 17 October 1872 in Villisca, Iowa. At the age of 8 "Nate" came with his parents to establish a residence in Oketo, Kansas. It was here that he spent his early years. For a period of 14 years, he was engaged in the combined business of merchant and Postmaster. He married first Cynthia Delair, and they had a son and a daughter. After resigning from the Postal Service, he and his second wife, Magdalena, moved to St. Joseph, Missouri, where he engaged in the wholesale business. In April 1914 he came to Bigelow State Bank, founded by his father. In 1917 Nate and Magdalena took over the Bank, and continued to manage it until his death in 1946. Surmounting many years of adversity, they built one of the strongest banking institutions in Marshall County. In addition to the Bank, Nate owned and operated a grain and stock farm near Bigelow, Kansas. He was active in the Republican party, holding a post on the Bigelow Township Committee for 30 years.
- Lulu Ethel Brubaker, born 17 July 1875 on a farm, near Villisca, Iowa. She worked in the Bigelow State Bank with her father and brother, Nathan. She moved to Morenci, Arizona, where she ran a boarding house for employees of Phelps Dodge Co. and Anaconda Copper Co., prior to and during World War I. She operated an apartment house in Long Beach, California, where she met and married Mr. Sommerville, her 4$^{th}$ husband. After divorcing Mr. Summerville, she and her sister, Imogene & her husband, Raymond Colton, operated Motels at Baker and Bend, Oregon. Lulu is shown in Picture (115). She may have married four times, but only the Summerville marriage is known. She had no children.

*Lulu Brubaker*

- John Lyman (Bob) Brubaker, born 9 April 1877 in Villisca, Iowa. He married Edna Scott in July 1903, and ran a General Store. He was an Insurance Agent and a Border Inspector at the port of entry in Marysville, KS.
- Harlowe Emerson Brubaker, born 5 March 1879 in Eldena, Illinois. He Married Inez Drake and was an accountant and auditor for Phelps Dodge Company in Arizona for 42 years, and at one time was County Treasurer (or Assessor) in Clifton, Arizona. When he retired they moved to El Paso, Texas.
- Emet Hill Brubaker, born 1 March 1881 in Eldena, Illinois. Emet operated a General Store in Oketo, Kansas, but was a professional baseball pitcher. He also had a talent for music, playing both the violin and mandolin by ear. He went to Morenci, Arizona, where he played baseball for the Phelps Dodge mining company team. While there, Myrtie E. Fulton came and they married in Lordsburg, New Mexico, 14 June 1903. Their family and history is in Chapter 2, Section 2.
- Imogene Brubaker, born 24 October 1887 in Lanham, Kansas. Imogene spent her early years in Kansas, and married Howell Raymond Colton 24 September 1910. After marriage they lived in Payette, Idaho, until 1941 (except for 5 years in Arizona). Ray was a

partner with Imogene's brother Emet Hill Brubaker in the Brubaker & Colton garage and Nash automobile dealership in Payette. From Payette they moved around Oregon (Portland, Lebanon, Baker & Bend). Imogene was a member of the Baker Christian Church and a 38-year member of Payette's Harmony Rebekah Lodge #22. Their children: Armin Vere Colton born about 1912; Anna Doris Colton born about 1914; Hillis Ray Colton died in infancy 1918; Harold C. Colton born about 1920; Myron Dale Colton born about 1924; Clifford N. Colton born about 1926. Vere served in the U. S. Army. And Harold, Myron and Clifford were in the Navy during WWII. Myron was missing in action at the Battle of Savo Island.

- Scott Brubaker, born 17 February 1889, married Genevieve Wilde, and they went to Morenci, Arizona, where he worked in the accounting department of the General Store. The store was first owned by Denver Copper Company, and later by Phelps Dodge Company. Scott was an excellent baseball player, and played in Morenci and Payette. They had two sons: Jerome and Raymond. The family moved to Payette, Idaho, due to their son's, Jerome, illness in the Morenci climate. In Payette, Scott worked for Denny Fruit Company, then F. H. Hogue Company. Scott was chief accountant and handled Hogue fruit sales throughout the United States. He retired in 1961. Scott and Genevieve are shown in Pictures (116) and (117).

*Scott Brubaker.*

*Genevieve (Wilde) Brubaker.*

Anna Marie (Hill) Brubaker died 15 November 1944, nine months past her 90th birthday. A. H. attended his great grandson's, Leland Emet Bolt, high school graduation in 1946. He lived until 24 May 1949. That was seven months past his 102nd birthday.

The mustached, silver - haired A. H. is shown in Picture (118) at about 100 years of age. He attributed his long life to clean living. He neither smoked nor drank, and maintained regular hours. His family believed another factor in his long life is his remarkable sense of humor - a dormant attribute in many people.

*Alvah Humbert Brubaker, the Centurian.*

# References

The author had many contacts with his great-grandfather. A. H. lived in in nearby Payette. The following references were also used:

1. Marysville, Kansas, Daily News, Monday 28 Dec 1910; Bigelow Bank Robbery - Cashier A. H. Brubaker and Daughter, Lulu, have tussle with Robber.
2. Marysville, KS, Advocate Newspaper 20 October 1946; Obituary, Nathan A. Brubaker
3. Foster, Emma E., History of Marshall County, Kansas; It's People, Industries and Institutions, B. F. Brown & Co., 1917, Chapter XIX Banks and Banking.
4. The Idaho Statesman (print edition) Boise, Idaho, June 1948, A. H. Brubaker Hale at 101 Years.
5. The Idaho Statesman (print edition) Boise, Idaho, 25 May 1949, Payette Man, Long Term Idahoan, Succumbs at Home. 102.
6. Letter, Harlowe E. Brubaker to Iris (Brubaker) Mordhorst 29 April 1965
7. Kindig, Lucille (Brubaker), "BRUBAKER FAMILY HISTORY" - 1979 Update, by Lucille Kindig, Page2.
8. Bolt, Fern (Brubaker) Bolt, Brubaker Family Notes 1966
9. Obituary, Imogene (Brubaker) Colton, Baker City Herald, Baker City, Oregon.
10. Interview of Myrtie (Fulton) Brubaker, and Brubaker & Hill Family Data sheets.

# SECTION 4

# The George Reynolds Fulton & Eliza Ann Woodcock Family

George Reynolds Fulton was a descendant of sterling New York Ancestry. Both his parents, John and Sally M. (Greene) Fulton, were natives of New York, and John was born near Syracuse.

George's parents instilled in him a keen sense of honor, integrity and thrift. He had a common school education. At 21, he was established as a merchant in Ashton, Illinois. The business prospered, and at 23 he bought a partnership in C. W. Barber's general merchandise store in Ogle County, Illinois.

Eliza Ann Woodcock was a lady of superior culture and refinement. She completed education in Worcester, Massachusetts, public schools and at an excellent Worcester private seminary. While visiting her sister in Illinois, she met and married George Reynolds Fulton 21 August 1861 (or 21 July 1861 see below date of 1st Battle of Bull Run). Could be date of license versus date of marriage. Eliza was an English girl, who liked her afternoon tea and cakes. Her marriage to George Fulton was on the day of the first Battle of Bull Run. It was understood that her family did not approve of her marriage to Mr. Fulton, and that is probably the reason little more is known of her family. On her wedding day Eliza presented an American flag to a Civil War regiment from her home town. Picture (119) is an early picture of Eliza.

*Eliza Ann (Woodcock) Fulton.*

George left the Barber store partnership in 1865, and partnered with C. E. Adams in a Dement (now Creston), Illinois store. In 1868 he moved the family to Kansas. He and Eliza homesteaded 377 acres (Section 34, Oketo Township) in Marshall County. In 1917 they had 68 head of cattle, 30 horses and two car-loads of hogs. Indians were frequent visitors to the farm. They were not unfriendly, usually looking through windows to see what food they could get. In addition to farming, the Fultons raised race horses and entered races. They were members and supporters of the Presbyterian Church. George served on the School Board, and once was Township Treasurer. Originally, George affiliated with the Republican Party. Later, he was prominent in the Union Labor Party, and was a delegate to their County conventions. In 1903 George and Eliza retired, sold the farm and moved to Payette, Idaho. Picture (120) is an older picture of George. They both died in Payette, but were returned to Marysville, Kansas, for burial. They had invested wisely in Payette properties, owning about ¼ of a city block. The property was inherited by their son, Charles, and daughter, Myrtie Edna.

*George Reynolds Fulton*

*Leoline Susan Fulton*

Their children were:

- Adopted son – Nathan Todd Fulton, about whom there was no further information.
- Leoline Susan Fulton, born 4 March 1862 and died in 1921. She had a brief marriage, and no children. She had a natural musical talent. She lived most of her life with her parents, moving with them to Payette, Idaho in 1903. Leoline, nicknamed "Lena", is shown in Picture (121). She was a milliner and a perfectionist.
- George Robert Fulton, born 5 June 1863 and died in 1879.

- Charles Sanford Fulton, born 28 July 1871 and died 28 January 1947. He rode race horses for his father. He was a painter and paper hanger by trade. He and his wife, Gertrude Imogene (Chapman) Fulton, lived most of their lives in Payette, Idaho.
- Roy John Fulton 27 February 1876 – 7 February 1877
- Female Child, born 19 March 1878 & died in infancy.
- Clifford Everett Fulton, born 17 May 1879 & died in infancy.
- Myrtie Edna Fulton, born 23 August 1881 and died in Jun 1971, married Emet Hill Brubaker. Myrtie is shown in Picture (122). See Chapter 2, Section 2, for their family.

*Myrtie Edna Fulton.*

## References:

1. Portrait and Biographical Album, Marshall Co., Kansas; Chapman Brothers, Chicago, 1889.
2. Forter, Emma E.; History of Marshall County Kansas, It's People, Industries and Institutions; B. F. Brown & Co., Indianapolis, Indiana; 1917.
3. Account by Myrtie Fulton and her Fulton Family by Iris E Brubaker Mordhorst (Ref 58).
4. Letter, Gladys Fulton to Fern (Brubaker) Bolt re: George Reynolds Fulton and Eliza Ann Woodcock descendants.

5. 1880 U.S. Census, Kansas, Marshall County, Page 81 Schedule; Original Manuscript.

6. Obituary, Mrs. George R. Fulton, Marysville, Kansas, Advocate - Democrat (print edition) November 1, 1917.

7. Headstones, Marysville, KS, Cemetery, George Reynolds Fulton Family, Photographs.

8. Author's Interview with Myrtie Edna (Fulton) Brubaker.

# CHAPTER 2

## The Parents

# SECTION 1

# The Benjamin D. Bolt & Lotta E. Zimmerman Family

Benjamin Darius Bolt received a formal school education, through one year of high school, at Red Oak, Iowa. He read everything he could get. He established a small library, and through constant reading obtained a well-rounded education. His father took him and his brother, Albert, to San Francisco, California, when Ben was 15. He worked in a store there for two years. Returning to Red Oak, he worked in the dry goods stores of George K. Powers for 8 years. In 1893 he established the Bolt Shoe Store on the East side of the square in the center of Red Oak. During the next 17 years this business became one of the leading shoe stores in Southwestern Iowa. Picture (316) shows Ben in 1898.

*Benjamin Darius Bolt*

Lotta Ebourne Zimmerman was educated in New York public Schools, and in 1895 graduated from the Griffith Institute in Springville, New York. Picture (317) shows Lotta about 1897. She taught school near Springville for a term, then was hired to teach 2ⁿᵈ grade at Lincoln School Red Oak, Iowa. She and Benjamin Darius Bolt married in 1898 and began raising a family. Leland Eddy Bolt (Picture [318]) was born 15 July 1899, Benjamin Draper Bolt (Picture 319) born 15 July 1901 and Margaret Adelle Bolt Picture (320) born10 March 1905.

*Lotta Elbourne (Zimmerman) Bolt.*

*Leland Eddy Bolt about 24 years of age.*

*Benjamin Draper Bolt about 21 years of age.*

*Margaret Adelle Bolt about 18 years of age.*

Ben was diagnosed with allergic reactions to the Iowa environment, and advised to leave the area. In 1909 he and Lotta moved the family to a farm outside Freewater, Oregon, where he raised fruit (primarily apples) and engaged in wholesale and retail fruit sales. Later, Ben worked in a shoe store in Walla Walla, Washington. The farm work was then largely done by his son, Leland, with assistance from Brother Ben and Sister Margaret. Their daughter, Martha (see Picture [321]) was born at Freewater 19 April 1919.

*Martha Eleanor Bolt about 18.*

By the time Martha was born in 1919, Leland had been drafted into the Army. Benjamin Draper Bolt had completed high school, and after a year in college, gone to Washington, D.C. In 1922 Margaret Adelle had graduated from the new Mc Loughlin High School in Milton-Freewater and left for College in McMinnville, Oregon. After her first year she transferred to Willamette University in Salem, Oregon.

Ben was tall (6 foot), trim and erect. He was true gentleman, who never used profanity. His command of the English language was effectively applied to most situations. In cases of short exclamation of disappointment, he used the word "mercy"! This strong and hard-working man enjoyed life and his family, including the grandchildren. He was a Christian man and faithful member of the Milton-Freewater First Baptist Church, having helped build the Church. He taught Sunday School and served in church offices. When he died he was Deacon Emeritus. He also served on the board of Mc Laughlin Union High School for 8 years, and Clerk of the Ferndale School District for several terms.

Lotta is shown about 1942 in Picture (322). She was a strong and disciplined lady, able to manage her family and support the couple's farm enterprises. They always had a cow, and she made her own butter, skimmed milk and cottage cheese. She raised vegetables and flowers every year. It was a treat to visit Lotta and Ben, because the chicken and garden food was so delicious.

Everything was always fresh, because, for most of her life there was only a naturally vented cooling cabinet and a small ice box. Ben executed the chicken and she picked the vegetables just before the meal. It wasn't until the late 1940s that she had a refrigerator and freezer. Lotta had a wonderful command of the English language, and effectively applied it to any situation. This strong and hard working woman enjoyed life and her family, including the grandchildren. They always had chickens, and Sunday usually included a chicken dinner in a nearby park (Pendleton, Oregon or Walla Walla, Washington) with Ben's sister, Myrtle, and her husband, Fred Swanson, and children. They lived in nearby Pendleton, Oregon. She was a strong Christian and faithful member of the Milton-Freewater Baptist Church. She was a Deaconess of the church, and she prepared the communion bread, provided flowers and food for special occasions.

*Lotta Elbourne (Zimmerman) Bolt.*

About 1930, Ben established a packing house to clean and pack his fruit, which sold near and far. He sold (door to door) in local towns. For sales further away, he packed a railroad car of apples and shipped it to a first destination (e.g. Laramie, Wyoming), where he met the shipment and sold some of the apples. He'd ship the remaining apples on East, meet the shipment and sell more. The process took him through Iowa and often on to Chicago. Along with farming, Ben was a bookkeeper at Lamb Fruit Company and managed the Freewater Box Company until it was destroyed by fire in 1923

During the summer school vacations, the grandchildren came to visit grandpa and grandma. When their first grandchild, Leland Emet Bolt, was born in 1928, his mother, Fern, brought him to visit his grandparents. She returned to the farm with him for a few days each year, until he was old enough to stay by himself. His parents then drove him to the farm or met the grandparents in an intervening town to accept the boy. Other grand-children (like Donald, Ann and Carol Denman) frequently visited their grandparents, and occasionally Benjamin Hamele Bolt, Benjamin Draper Bolt's son, visited. The grandparents were amazed at their huge appetites. Ben told of his grandson, Donald K. Denman, who just having finished lunch, asked what we were having for supper!

Ben and Lotta were able to attend the wedding of their grandson, Leland Emet Bolt, and Jaqueline Joyce Barker, in 1952.

The family of Ben and Lotta's first son, Leland, and his wife, Fern Leoline Brubaker, is detailed in Chapter 3.

Benjamin Draper Bolt attributes his middle name to the Drapers, who were close friends of his parents in Iowa. He graduated from Ferndale High School, in a class of four. He went to Linville College in McMinnville, Oregon, majoring in Journalism. After two years, the urge to go other places and do other things was overwhelming. He drove his Ford Model T to the train station, abandoned it there, and traveled to Washington, D.C.

Ottamar Hamele, husband of Benjamin Draper Bolt's aunt, Mattie (Zimmerman) Hamele, was living in Washington D.C. Ottamar was an attorney and Chief Council of Bureau of Reclamation. He was very helpful to Ben and the Bolt family in general. Ben got a job with Shell Oil Company. While employed by Shell, he took a correspondence course in accounting, and was then able to work in their accounting department. He later worked for the F.B.I., requiring him to get employment, as an accountant, at suspect firms to determine their illegal activities. In doing so, he was often treated well by his employers. It bothered him to have to "blow the whistle" on them.

Ben then went to California. Picture (323) shows Ben in 1932, while a student at University of California. He worked in the Standard Oil Company accounting department to finance his work at the University's School of Forestry. He earned his Forestry B.S. degree in 1933.

*Benjamin Draper Bolt as a student at University of California.*

Laura Elizabeth Mead, born 15 August 1899, attended schools in South Dakota. At the age of 17, she had been recruited to teach grades 1 through high school in a South Dakota one-room schoolhouse. In 1928 she earned a Bachelor of Arts degree from University of South Dakota. She worked as a dietician at Chicago's Cook County Hospital, then traveled west to do graduate work at University of California, Berkeley. Laura (shown in Picture [324]) met and married Benjamin Draper Bolt 31 October 1933. Their son, Benjamin Hamele Bolt, was born 27 September 1934 in Oakland, California. His middle name was to honor his uncle, Ottamar Hamele. While Ben's Forest Service career was brief, Ben jr. said his earliest memories were of living in the woods in a big tent, and doing a lot of moving. Ben and his son spent a lot of time together in the woods and mountains over the course of the rest of his life, and he told his son many stories from his forestry days. Those were the type-mapping times, and his son especially liked those assignments. Picture (325) shows Ben and his mule out working in the forests.

*Laura (Meade) Bolt about 1929.*

*Ben and his mule at work in the forests.*

The problem with Ben's forestry career was that Laura could not pursue her career while he worked that job. She had been a stay-at-home mother, but now wanted to pursue her passion for influencing personal nutrition. Ben quit the U.S. Forest Service and took an accounting job with the California State Board of Equalization. This job enabled his wife to work for the Kern County Health Department as a public health nutritionist.

In 1937 Laura joined the Kern County Health Department as Dietician and Field Nutritionist. Her chief undertaking was to improve the lot of the Midwest "Dust Bowl" immigrants to California, who were camped in various locations. Conditions under which these desperate people lived were vividly portrayed in John Steinbeck's "The Grapes of Wrath". Although her work with the "Dust Bowl" folks ended with the start of World War II, Laura and Ben had settled in Bakersfield and the rest of her career was devoted to Kearn County nutrition. Picture (326) is a 1940 picture of Laura.

*Laura (Meade) Bolt about 1940.*

About 1955 Ben left the State Board of Equalization and established his own accounting business.

A local area news article described Laura's professional passion work best, saying "Laura Bolt, nutritionist of the Kern County Health Department, was guest speaker at the recent Sunset PTA meeting. Her topic of discussion was the building of a healthy body through use of high nutrient foods during the period of growth." Laura had the perfect demonstration of her concept of nutrition and exercise building healthy bodies. Her son, Benjamin Hamele Bolt, was over 6 foot tall and strong. He was an outstanding swimmer, regularly competing in High school competition. Picture (327) shows his high school swim team. He is front row, third from left.

*The Bakersfield Swim Team about 1951.*

In addition to her Health Department work, Laura started several organizations. She helped form the Bakersfield Art Association, and started one of the County's first weight loss groups, with emphasis on nutrition and similar to "Weight Watchers". She organized a club for single adults, and named it the Mead Club for her maiden name. Though her final years were clouded by dementia, she lived a long and productive 96 years. She died in 1995.

Ben had an interest in botany, and enjoyed nature. He was an avid reader of historical information, and had a collection of classical music recordings. He could read and understand Greek, German, Spanish and Latin. He was also a successful stock market investor. During his final few years he was quite feeble, but of strong mind. His grandson, Mitchell Benjamin Bolt, stayed with him to ensure his safety and comfort. Ben never retired from his accounting business. When he died in 1992 he was still serving one remaining client. (UCB Forestry Magazine).

Margaret Adelle Bolt is shown in Picture (328). Her brothers, Leland and Benjamin, convinced her to go to college. She attended College in Mc Minnville, Oregon, for a year, then took 8 years to graduate from

Willamette University in 1930. She financed her college studies by working at the Oregon Department of Motor Vehicles and as manager of her sorority. She stayed out of school occasionally to accumulate finances to continue. Upon graduation, she had been Vice President of the Student Body, French Scholar her senior year, Manager of the Delta Phi Sorority for 2 years, and Maid to the May Queen. Following graduation, she was an Assistant French teacher at Willamette University, and did stenographic work at the Oregon State Capital.

*Margaret Bolt about high school age.*

At a glee club rehearsal, Margaret met Kenneth G. Denman, who was attending Law School and coaching football at Willamette University. It was there that Margaret Bolt acquired the nickname "Bennie Bolt", derived from the old song "Sweet Alice Ben Bolt". Ken fell in love with Bennie Bolt, and that was her nickname ever after. Ken and Bennie became engaged. After a call to her parents for parental concurrence, her father called his oldest son, Leland, and asked that he determine if Ken was a suitable husband. Ken and Leland both loved the outdoors, fishing and hunting. Leland gave a strong O. K. Ken and Margaret married in 1931. As seen in Picture (329), they went camping and fishing on their honeymoon. Margaret (Bennie) lost Ken's favorite fishing fly, but the marriage survived - good omen.

*Ken & Margaret camping out.*

Kenneth Denman was born and raised in Corvallis, Oregon. Graduating from Corvallis High School in 1923, and from Oregon Agricultural College (later became Oregon State University) in 1927. He was a varsity football player at OAC, and a member of the Phi Delta Theta fraternity. He earned his law degree from Willamette University College of Law in 1930, and established his practice in Medford, Oregon. Margaret supported him in his law practice, while raising their three children. Their children were: Donald Kenneth Denman (born 13 June 1933), Margaret Ann Denman (born 17 October 1935 and Carol Louise Denman (born 31 January 1938). Ken was a dedicated sportsman, and taught his children fishing and hunting, as well as water sports and skiing. He was a good steward of the public lands and the world of wild life, serving a number of years on the Oregon State Fish and Wildlife Commission. Picture (330) is a picture of Ken in 1952.

*Kenneth G. Denman in 1952.*

Margaret's brother, Leland, visited the Denmans often, and went fishing with Ken. Picture (471) is Lee and Ann Denman, exhibiting his catch of the day.

*Lee, Ann and the fish.*

Ken lived to see his son, Donald K. Denman, graduate from law school in 1962 and return to join his law firm. But, Ken's untimely death in 1962 ended those plans.

After Ken's death, Bennie married John Horner (born 8 March 1906 in Simi Valley, California) 24 August 1963. He was also widowed, and a family friend. John was a retired Superintendent at a large electrical company in Los Angeles, California. In retirement, he moved to Oregon and raised cattle on his Applegate River ranch, near Jacksonville, Oregon. John and Bennie enjoyed traveling, often on ocean cruises with her brother, Leland, and his wife, Fern. The ranch is a special place for all the Denman family. Margaret died 26 May 1998 in Medford, Oregon, and John died 14 April 1999 in Jacksonville, Oregon.

Donald K. Denman was 6' 3" tall, and graduated from Medford High School, where he played football, basketball and baseball. He attended Oregon State College (later named Oregon State University). He and Carol were the third generation of Denmans to graduate from Oregon State. Don, like his father, was a member of the Phi Delta Theta fraternity. Don was in Air Force ROTC at Oregon State and, upon graduation in 1955, served on active duty as a navigator for tankers refueling aircraft over the Atlantic Ocean.

After graduation from Willamette University Law School in 1962, Don took over his father's practice. Don, shown in Picture (331), and John P. "Jack" Cooney formed a law partnership that lasted for over 25 years, until Jack became a Federal Magistrate. Don then merged his practice with Stuart Foster's law firm and practiced law as Foster Denman, until his retirement in 2008. Don also served as a pro-tem circuit court judge during this period. He was an active and involved community and state leader. He served on the boards and as chairman of many groups, including the Girls Community Club, Friends of the Library, KSYS Public Television, Jackson County Community Concert Association, Medford Rotary Club, and the Craterian Ginger Rogers Theater. In 1967 he was selected as one of Oregon's Ten Outstanding Young Men by the Oregon Jaycees. He was active in the Oregon Bar Association, serving as past president of Jackson County Bar Association and as chairs of the Oregon State Bar Legal Ethics Committee (Estate Planning section) and Disciplinary Review Board.

*Donald K. Denman, the Medford Attorney.*

An active conservationist, Don served as vice-chair of the Bureau of Land Management District Advisory Board, and the local Izaak Walton League. He followed in his father's footsteps, serving almost 10 years on the Oregon Fish and Wildlife Commission.

Don married Sandra Kerr Daley 7 February 1959 in Bath, Maine. Their first child, Donna Kay Denman (born 2 May 1967 in Medford, Oregon) married Richard Charles Irwin of Bridgton, Maine, 7 November 1998. Their second daughter, Diane Reed Denman (born 3 September 1970 in Medford) married Theodore (Todd) Courtland Johanson Jr. 28 November 1998 in Georgetown, Maine. Diane and Todd's children are: Carter Reed Johanson (born 28 May 2003) and Cole Bolt Johanson (born 27 November 2005.

Don and Sandra divorced about 1978. In 1984, Don married Kristy Virginia Henshaw at Medford, Oregon. She was an elementary teacher in the Medford District, then a Flight Attendant for Continental Airlines (now merged with United). Don and Kristy were members of the First Presbyterian Church of Medford. They served as Elders and assumed leadership roles in nearly every church committee, and sang in its Chancel Choir. In retirement they continued to live in the Cady Lane home and enjoyed a vacation home in Gold Beach, Oregon. As Don's health deteriorated, they moved to a home in Medford. Don died 21 November 2015 at age 82.

Ken and Margaret's daughter, Margaret Ann Denman (born 17 October 1935) used her middle name, Ann. She graduated from Medford High School, then from Willamette University, with a degree in Biology. She earned a Nursing Degree from the University of Oregon. She worked as a Registered Nurse at Dornbecker Hospital in Portland, Oregon, then at Roseville Hospital, near her home in Fair Oaks, California.

Ann married Clarence W. Hultgren (born 17 August 1930 in Eugene, Oregon) 16 August 1958 in Medford, Oregon. Their children: Julianne Adelle Hultgren (born 3 March 1964 in Portland, Oregon) and Jennifer Ellen Hultgren (born 6 February 1966 in Portland, Oregon). Julianne (called Julie) married Chris Garrett (born 2 April 1965 in Placerville, California). He died 18 May 2011. Julie and Chris' children are: Dillon Scott Garrett (born 15 June 2001) and Sierra DiAnn Garrett (born 23 June 2003). Jennifer (called Jenny) married Jason Horn. Though divorced. Ann and Clarence remained friends.

In retirement, Ann was in bonsai horticulture, growing and serving in bonsai organizations. She traveled to shows in Japan and other countries.

Ken & Margaret's daughter, Carol Louise Denman, was born 31 January 1938 in Medford, and graduated from Medford High School. She married Montgomery Glenn Holst (born 24 August 1938) 15 September 1956 at the First Presbyterian Church in Medford, Oregon. They both graduated from Oregon State University. Carol finished her degree work after their first son, Brad, was born, then completed her Master's Degree in teaching.

In 1966, Monty's steel industry job took the family to Placentia, Orange County, in Southern California. Carol taught Business Education Technology at Valencia High School for 31 years. Monty had a State Farm Insurance agency in Fullerton for 29 years. Monty and Carol's children are: Brad Montgomery Holst (born 8 February 1957 in Redding, California), Margaret Dee Holst (born 27 April 1960 in Corvallis, Oregon) and David Glenn Holst (born 8 November 1962 in Portland, Oregon).

Brad married Diane Marie Joyner 5 January 1991 in Orange County, California. Their children are: Taylor Denman Holst (born 9 July 1994) and Patrick Glenn Holst (born 4 June 1996).

Margaret Dee (Mardee) Holst married Troy Steven Ford 23 March 1985 in Placentia, California. Their children are: Steven Troy Ford (born 9 January 1986 in Kennett Square, Pennsylvania), Thomas Glenn Ford (born 11 June 1988 and died 12 October 1988 in Kennett Square, Pennsylvania). Mathew Glenn Ford (born 9 November 1991) and David Howard Ford (born 9 November 1993) in Clovis, California.

David Holst married Lori Christine Hertel (born 31 January1963 in Ventura, California) 21 December 1987. David and Lori's children are: John Westerfeld Holst (born 2 December 1992 in Ventura County, California), and identical twin daughters; Christine Carol Holst and Katherine Rose Holst (born 17 July 1995 in Ventura, California).

Monty and Carol purchased the Horner ranch in 1977. John and Carol's Mother, Margaret, continued to live there into the 1990s. Monty and Carol moved there when both were retired in 2001, and were active in the Medford community and the First Presbyterian Church.

Martha Eleanor Bolt, was born at Freewater, Oregon, 29 April 1919. By that time her brothers had left home and her sister, Margaret, left when Martha was 3. Martha attended Ferndale Grade School and the new McLoughlin Union High School. Every summer her nephew, Emet (brother Leland's son), came to stay with the family. Martha became closer to him than to her brothers and sister. Those summers were extremely hot in the valley, so Martha and her mother moved up in the Blue Mountains and their cabin at Cold Springs. It was cool and with abundant wildlife. The cold spring flowed within 40 feet of the cabin. Her dad and Emet worked the farm during the week, and joined Martha and her mother on weekends. When people asked Ben what he did for food during their stay at the farm, he said they lived on roots and herbs. Sometimes the Milton-Freewater Baptist Church had picnic services on a nearby green in those mountains. The family gathered mushrooms and huckleberries too. Once or twice a summer Martha and other kids in the camp would hike down the hill to Bingham springs now known as the Bar M Ranch. They would start in early morning, swim all day in the hot springs. Going back up was always exhausting, and they had to make it before dark. The cabin dated back to the late 1920s, when Ben had a sawmill in the area. After the mill burned, the owner of this forested area allowed the Bolt Cold Springs cabin to remain. It was a special place in tall timber that the family had enjoyed for decades - riding horses, hiking, picking huckleberries, gathering mushrooms.

The Milton-Freewater Baptist Church was a big part of the Bolt family life. It was here that Martha met a handsome boy named Bardel M. VanDonge Jr. He was born in Nolin, Oregon 15 March 1918. The family was living on a large farm near Cove, Oregon, where Bardel jr. and his two brothers rode to school on one horse. The family moved to Walla Walla, but attended this church, due to a connection with the pastor. Bardel had regularly dated another girl, but Martha extracted him (her words) by making herself very available. Martha was planning a party for the Baptist Youth Fellowship and she specifically invited Bardel. That was their first date. Later Martha introduced her friend Esther Cole (from Umapine) to Bardel's brother, Millerd, and those two later married. Dates included picnics at Immigrant Park, Liberty Theater movies, and hikes at the Bolt Cold Springs cabin. Her mother occasionally had Martha and Bardel take her nephew, Emet, (visiting from Idaho) with them to the movies when he was there for the summer.

After High school, Martha completed a post-graduate course at Loughlin Union High School, and was very interested the medical profession. Once, while a relative was visiting at the Cold Springs cabin, the lady's jaw locked open during a laughing session. Martha got out her book and applied the "unlocking procedure". It didn't work, so they drove to Weston, Oregon, to see an MD. He did the same as Martha had tried and the jaw was released. Martha just had not pushed hard enough.

Picture (332) shows Martha about 1940. Her brother, Ben, had worked in Washington, D. C., for some time, and convinced her to go there and get training. With help from Uncle Ottamar Hamele, she entered St. Elizabeth's Hospital School of Nursing. This was a large government psychiatric hospital. Uncle Ottamar, the Chief Council of the U. S. Bureau of Reclamation, took care of Martha and became a key figure in her life. She lived in the dormitory but Uncle Ottamar, having no children of his own, made sure she was cultured. He took her to the theater often - Broadway plays and musicals. He took her to one of the inaugural balls for President Franklin D. Roosevelt, buying her a fancy gown for the event.

*Martha Eleanor Bolt about 20 years of age.*

Bardel followed Martha back East, and found work during World War II for the Glen L. Martin Aircraft Company in Baltimore, Maryland. Following two years at St. Elizabeth's, Martha went to Jersey City Medical Center for surgical and pediatric experience. After a few months she decided it was time to marry. She and Bardel were married 23 November 1941 in Baltimore's Hamilton Baptist Church, by Rev. Otis Reade. Baltimore became home for the new Van Donge family. Picture (333) shows Susan with her parents soon after her birth in 1942. Robert was born there 4 March 1944 in Baltimore.

*Bardel, Martha and their first child, Susan.*

When the war was ending, they moved back to the old Van Donge farm in Walla Walla Valley. There were wartime imposed problems with moving across the country. First, they had to get federal permission, which required assurance they had a job where they were going. That was easy, because the Van Donge parents surely needed help on the farm. The next problem was finding a car that would make the trip. During the war years, few cars were produced for civilian use. Most of those were taken by priority for businesses involved in the war effort. Uncle Ottamar had mentioned, within her hearing of Eleanor Roosevelt, that his niece needed to drive across country and was looking for a car. Eleanor sold him hers. The third obstacle was gasoline stamps. Wartime rationing was still in effect. Gas stamps were required at every refueling. Relatives and friends in Walla Walla and Baltimore donated ration stamps. They drove from Baltimore in the Eleanor Roosevelt car. The only thing Martha kept from it was a little cut glass bud vase that was in a holder in the car.

The senior Van Donges retired, and Bardel entered into Van Donge Brothers farming partnership with his brother, Millerd. Carolee and Connie were born in 1947 and 1952.

Martha started her own dog-breeding and showing business. This was a strong part of her life at the time. The kennel was called Sugar Acre Cockers, because Van Donge Brothers farm was mainly raising sugar beets.

She bred and sold Cocker Spaniels, boarded a few other dogs occasionally, and showed her dogs at various dog shows, as far away as Lewiston, Idaho.

Martha developed a strong interest in antiques. She bought her first antiques with what she called her "puppy money." It was unusual for women to have their own business, but these things were all very important to her. She began dealing in buying and selling reclaimed merchandise.

Martha also cared for foster babies. They were newborns just out of the hospital and before they were placed for adoption. Martha named the babies and sometimes the adoptive parents continued that name. She had one for 6 months, until she (Sally) was placed. That really bothered her to part with the child, so she quit being the temporary baby mom.

Martha's father, Benjamin Darius Bolt, died 1 January 1956. His grave is in Mountain View Cemetery at Walla Walla, Washington. Martha & Bardel helped sell the Bolt family farm and moved her mother, Lotta, to a mobile home on the Van Donge farm. Martha and Bardel and their children enabled her to live in a pleasant environment until she too passed away 11 January 1964. Her grave is along-side her Ben in Walla Walla's Mountain View Cemetery

Van Donge Brothers farming partnership was quite profitable, and the wives were key partners in farm operations and raising the children. Bardel and Martha attended Bolt reunions in California, which began in Toluca Lake, California, in 1969. Reunions continued on alternate years at other places in California, Washington, and Oregon. Bardel died 6 September 2001 in Walla Walla. Martha kept on attending the reunions through the 2006 reunion, hosted by her daughter, Carolee, and husband Larry White in Walla Walla, Washington. At that reunion she again connected with her nephew, Leland Emet Bolt, and recalled the wonderful times at the Walla Walla Park with her parents and her aunt, Myrtle, and Uncle, Fred, Swanson. Martha died 30 March 2008. .

Susan Van Donge was a traveler, living in San Francisco, Hawaii and other places in California. Picture (336) is Susan, her stepson, Vincent, her son, Neils, and her husband, Neil Kirk. The picture was taken at their beautiful property up in the hills out of Willits, California. They were making improvements. Susan died 30 March 2006 in Naalehu, Hawaii.

*Susan with her husband, son and stepson.*

Robert Dean Van Donge was born 4 March 1944 in Baltimore, Maryland. He married Janet Mae Baker 27 June 1981in Walla Walla, Washington. Picture (334) is a marriage picture. Bob graduated from Central Washington College in 1966 and then taught elementary school for 42 years. Janet worked as a cardiovascular technician at the Walla Walla Clinic. Their children:

- Robert Mark VanDonge was born 4 August 1982. He graduated from Pomona College in 2005 and became a professional photographer in Walla Walla, Washington.
- Benjamin (Ben) Baker VanDonge was born 6 April 1987. He graduated from Whitman College in 2009. He married Katharine (Kate) Emily Pringle 4 June 2011. Kate was born 20 January 1989. Ben and Kate's daughter, Brienne Charlotte VanDonge, was born 21 July 2015. Picture (335) is Ben and Kate with daughter, Brienne

VanDonge in 2017. Ben is an elementary school teacher in Walla Walla. He plays the drums and guitar. He also cooks a great paella!

*Robert & Janet's marriage photo.*

*Brienne VanDonge and her parents 2017.*

Carolee Van Donge was born 2 April 1947 in Walla Walla, Washington. Some of her activities were horseback riding (member of an elite riding group that performed intricate drills at a fast canter), 4-H, Blue Birds and Campfire, Cheerleading and Baptist Youth Group. She graduated from Walla Walla High School in 1965, and married high school sweetie, Larry Merlen White 11 September 1965. They went to Corvallis, Oregon where Larry was a junior at Oregon State and Carolee was a freshman. Larry's senior year was at the medical school in Portland to finish his degree in Medical Technology. While in Portland, Carolee attended Portland Community College and worked for College Life (arranged by Cousin Carol's husband, Monty Holst).

Carolee and Larry lived rent free at the Portland Travelodge, as night managers. While there, they were visited by Cousin Lee and Jackie Bolt, who babysat for them so they could spend a day sightseeing. Larry graduated in 1967 and was employed by St. Mary's Hospital Laboratory in Walla Walla for one year. They moved to Wenatchee, Washington where Larry was a Medical Technician at Deaconess Hospital for 9 years. He also managed the book store at their church. He worked for Payless Drug Store, which moved them to Federal Way, Marysville and Bremerton (Washington) and later to Concord, California. They moved back to Walla Walla in 1989, and Larry became a Nursing Home Administrator. Carolee worked in special education for the school district. They retired in 2010 and Picture (337) shows them as they celebrated their 50th wedding anniversary in 2015.

*Larry & Carolee on their 50th wedding anniversary.*

Their Children:

- Tamara Christine White was born January 29, 1968 in Walla Walla. She graduated from Concord High in 1986 and then attended Mt. Diablo Community College. She graduated from University of California Santa Cruz and got a teaching degree from Warner Pacific College in Portland, Oregon. She married Christopher Van Hooser and taught in Tillamook, Oregon before her children were born. She is a substitute teacher in Hillsboro, Oregon. Their son, William Van Hooser, was born 1 October 1998. Today, he is a high school senior. Their daughter, Tessa Skye Van Hooser, was born 13 December 2001 and attends High School in Hillsboro.
- Kevin Christopher White was born 4 December 1970 in Wenatchee, Washington. He graduated from Concord High School in California where he was involved in the music program. Kevin graduated from Anderson University in 1994 and married Jennifer Campbell (born 23 May 1973) in Anderson, Indiana.

After graduation, Kevin was the music pastor in East Prairie, Missouri; Lima, Ohio; South Charleston, West Virginia; Colorado Springs, Colorado and Brookings, Oregon. He re-started a church in Redmond, Oregon. While in Redmond the family started a Children's Theater which made a tremendous impact on many children. 7 May 2017 they moved to Thailand to be missionaries.. Their children are Lydia Campbell-White (born 28 July 1996), Noah Campbell-White (born 5 June 1998), and Caleb Campbell-White (born 7 March 2001). Lydia is a nursing/music/missions student at Northwest Nazarene in Nampa, Idaho. Noah will attend Olivet in Chicago majoring in music and drama: Caleb Campbell-White is a home-schooled high school student. Picture (338) is the Kevin & Jennifer family ..

Caleb - Jeni - Kevin - Lydia - Noah

*The Kevin & Jennifer White family in 2017*

- Nathanael Thomas White was born 5 June_1975 in Wenatchee. Washington. He graduated from Walla Walla. High School and played football and baseball. He graduated from George Fox University where he played 2 years of baseball. He married Angela Grace Dean (born 22 September 1976). After Angela graduated from George Fox, Nathaniel joined the Air Force. After training at Vandenberg Air Force base in California he was assigned to a missile silo near

Great Fall, Montana. After various assignments in California and Colorado he retired as a Major. He is a substitute teacher and coach (football, wrestling and girls Lacrosse). Their children are: Taylor (born 27 October 1996) graduated from Pine Creek High School in 2015 where his football team won the state championship two years in a row. He also wrestled in the State Finals. He is a junior at Grand Canyon University majoring in Athletic Training. Jordan (born 21 October 1998) is a senior at Pine Creek High School. He is a swimmer and computer graphics designer. Brittney Nicole (born 15 November 2000) is a good athlete and plays Lacrosse. Ian Carter (born 19 March 2003). Picture (339) shows the family in 2016.

*Nathaniel & Angela White family 2016.*

- Jeremy Alan White was born 4 October 1977 in Wenatchee, Washington. He graduated from Walla Walla High School and played for the state football title in the Kingdome. He was recruited to play baseball at Pepperdine University. He graduated from Pepperdine in 2000, where he majored in sports medicine. After moving to Seattle he met and married Christine Zachary (born 26 March 1979). They have two children. London Elizabeth (born 10 April 2009) and Quinn Elise (born 23 October 2011). Jeremy is in computer software sales. Picture (340) shows Jeremy and Christine's family in 2016.

*The Jeremy & Christine White family.*

Connie, Martha and Bardel's youngest child, was born 13 May 1952 in Walla Walla, Washington. She was close to Grandma Bolt, who lived in a mobile home on the Van Donge property. Either Connie or Carolee slept at or near Grandma's mobile home at night.

Connie met Randy Rogers in 1968 at Walla Walla High School. She was attracted to music and he played drums in a local rock band. While preparing for her first date with him, Martha said "I hope he doesn't have long hair and wear those awful "Beatle boots." When she opened the door, there he stood, sporting both offending items! His smile and mellow personality saved the day. Randy's parents had owned a bakery and he had grown up learning the art and skill of baking. In 1972, he began work at a school in Alajuela, Costa Rica to teach baking skills. Connie flew from San Francisco, where she was living with her sister, Susan, to visit Randy in Alajuela. He had been the last person to get a travel visa to Costa Rica from Nicaragua before the devastating 1972 Managua earthquake. They married and lived there for about two years. Picture (342) is Randy and Connie in 2016. They lived in and drove an old Ford Econoline van to Walla Walla. Randy found an accounting job and Connie was an office and personnel manager. Their son, Andrew James Rogers, was born 25 June 1981 Walla Walla, WA.

*Randy and Connie at a social event!*

Connie inherited Martha's love of antiques, valued treasure items and memorabilia. Returning from Central America, broke and needing household furnishings, she went to yard sales. She picked up extra glassware and items found to be worth far more than the prices marked. She and Martha went to flea markets together. In the late 1970s, they did her first solo sales, along with Connie's friend. Connie went from having just a handful of sales per year to many more. She and her mother became partners in the enterprise. Martha eventually left the partnership and it became Connie's full-time occupation.

Randy and Connie had several businesses, including the commercial raising of alfalfa and bean sprouts. Their sprouts were distributed throughout Washington and Oregon. They purchased Rogers Bakery from his parents and combined the antiques, renaming it Rogers Bakery and Antiques. They sold it in 2000 and acquired Personal Touch Carpet Cleaning. Connie purchased the 1890 house that became Dietrich House Antiques, managing that and White Elephant Sales.

Randy & Connie's son Andrew James Rogers, was born 25 June 1981 in Clarkston, Washington, and graduated from Walla Walla College in 2007 with a business degree. Andrew was hired by Washington State Penitentiary in 2006 to supervise their bakery and work with the inmates in teaching various skills. That program has ceased, but he still supervised crews in the food service. Andrew was hired to work in Mozambique for two years, then returned to gather equipment and obtain funding for a farming operation in Mozambique. He married Nancy Rexinger 14 September 2014 in Idaho. He returned to Mozambique' then started work in Littleton, Colorado. Picture (343) is a 2016 picture..

*Andrew & Nancy soon after 'marriage.*

Picture (472) was taken when all four of Ben and Lotta's children were together for the last time, about 1985.

*The four children, together for the last time.*

# References:

1.  Bolt, Benjamin Darius, To My Children; unpublished working papers for his children documentation of his 1920 – 1950 family research (Ref. 14)
2.  Horton, A. J., The Descendants of Adam Rector, Carl J. Ward Printing, Buffalo, NY, 1915, pages 14 & 15 (Ref. 12)
3.  Denman, Kenneth, Telegram, Western Union, 31 January 1938; Birth of Baby Girl (Ref. 17)
4.  Interviews with Benjamin Darius Bolt, by Leland Emet Bolt 1950 (Ref. 31)
5.  Denman Family Data Sheets, by Kenneth G, Denman, with update by Donald K. Denman, dated 19 April 1997 (Ref.97)
6.  State of Washington, Bureau of Vital Statistics, Death Certificate, State file No. 2120 Lotta E. Bolt. (Ref. 156)
7.  Bolt, Benjamin Hamele; Biographies of himself, Benjamin Draper Bolt & Laura Elizabeth Mead, 8 October 2001. (Ref. 157)
8.  State of Oregon, Board of Health, Certificate of Death, Margaret A. Bolt, State Reg. No. 93, Local Reg. No. 21. (Ref. 160)
9.  State of Washington, Health Statistics, Death Certificate (File No. 1689), Benjamin Darius Bolt, signed 3 January 1956. (Ref. 161)
10. First Church of God, Walla Walla, WA, Wedding Invitation Janet M. Baker to Robert D. Van Donge, 27 June 1981. (Ref. 165)
11. Holst, Brad Montgomery; Brad, David and Margaret Dee (Holst) Ford, Holst Family data Sheets, undated. (Ref. 177)
12. Walla Walla Union Bulletin, January 2 1956; Pioneer Churchman, Ben Bolt, Dies (Ref. 88)
13. Walla Walla Union Bulletin, Walla Walla, WA, 12 January 1964, Mrs. Bolt dies at 89. [Obituary, Lotta E. Bolt (Ref. 182)]
14. Rogers, Drew, Bolt & Van Donge Family History, as told by Martha Eleanor (Bolt) Van Donge, Drew 10 June 2006. (Ref. 199)
15. Rogers, Drew, Bolt History dated 20 May 2008 (Ref. 187)
16. The Mac-Hi Messenger, published by students of McLoughlin High School, 7 May 1928; B. D. Bolt and other School Board Members. (Ref. 192)

17. Holst, Carol letter comments on Denman and Bolt Genealogy 2 November 2016 (Ref. 205)
18. Lee & Fern Book, Carol & Ann Denman comments 1st draft (Ref.205)
19. White, Carolee (Van Donge), letter to Leland E. Bolt, 8 May 2017; Re: Family (Ref. 206)
20. Van Donge, Robert Dean, letter to Leland E. Bolt, 1 May 2017; Re: Susan Van Donge family. (Ref. 207)
21. Van Donge, Robert Dean, Letters to Leland E. Bolt, 27 & 28 March & 2 May 2017; Re: Van Donge & Bolt Family History. (Ref. 208)
22. Connie (Van Donge) Rogers Letters to Leland E. Bolt, email 17 May 2017 Re: Her Rogers Family History. (Ref 209)

# SECTION 2

# The Emet Hill Brubaker & Myrtie Edna Fulton Family

Emet Hill Brubaker grew up in the mercantile store environment of his father, Alvah Humbert Brubaker, known as "A H". He taught Emet, his 4 brothers and two sisters the store and bank businesses and associated accounting and financial requirements. The five boys were good baseball players in school, and played as adults.

Initially, Emet ran a general store in Oketo, Kansas. He moved to Morenci, Arizona, about 1902, where he worked in the mining company store and earned extra money as a relief pitcher for the Company baseball team. In June, 1903, he arranged for Myrtie Edna Fulton, his girlfriend in Kansas, to come by train to Lordsburg, New Mexico, where they would be married. On the appointed day, Miss Fulton arrived at the Lordsburg train station, but Emet was not there! Morenci was about 55 miles away, and no regular transportation was available. The train back to Kansas would not leave for a couple of days, so Miss Fulton checked in at the hotel. Next day, while sitting on the hotel porch, she saw Emet walk by, and said "Emet Brubaker, what are you doing here?" Whatever he said must have been O. K., because they married in Lordsburg 14 June 1903. Their daughter, Hazel, was born 19 April 1904 in Morenci. Emet continued to work in the Company store and played baseball. When the baseball team was disbanded, he lost that extra pay and his job was no longer attractive. The family moved to Oketo, Kansas for a short time, where Emet managed a store. Their second daughter, Fern Leoline Brubaker, was born there 6 April 1906.

In 1910 the family moved to Idaho, where Emet homesteaded land near Parma, Idaho. Picture (**301**) shows Emet, Myrtie and daughter, Fern, around the homestead house. Emet worked in a grocery store to get money to farm. Iris Eliza Brubaker was born in Payette 25 September 1910. They were doing pretty well until 1916 when Emet was in a serious automobile accident. His injuries, included misalignment of his left eye. The rest of his life he wore glasses with the left lens frosted, to avoid double vision. They returned to the milder climate in Morenci for his recovery. Emet was able to work in the Denver Copper Company store, while recovering. Picture (302) shows Emet soon after the accident. No pictures before the accident have been found. Picture (303) shows their three daughters about 1917.

*Fern with parents on the old Homestead.*

*Emet after the 1916 Automobile Accident.*

*The 3 Brubaker sisters.*

In 1918 they moved to El Paso, TX, for a couple of months, then back to Payette, Idaho. Myrtie Edna (Fulton) Brubaker had music and piano training, and was quite talented. She gave piano lessons for a time, and worked with her daughters to instill music appreciation, and teach them to play the piano. She remembered a relative on her mother's side, Ezra Sawyer, who was instrumental in sending the second wireless message across the ocean. He lived in England, and was a member of the Queen's Court. Picture (304) shows Myrtie about 1938.

*Myrtie about 1938.*

The 1920s were particularly difficult for the family. Hazel and Fern were nearly the same age and needed changes of clothes. They were near the same size and could trade clothes and even shoes for the dances and dates.

Emet had experience in store management and financing. He learned to be a sign writer. He corrected people who said he was a sign painter, because he said most people can paint a sign, but only an artist can create consistent letters in a beautiful sign. In the 1920s and 30s Emet partnered with his brother-in-law and sister, Raymond and Imogene Colton, in an automobile service station on Payette's main street, doing business as Brubaker & Colton. They sold Veltex brand gasoline and serviced automobiles. For a time Emet was also the Nash franchised automobile dealer.

Emet was a self-taught carpenter and painter. Myrtie learned to help him hang wallpaper in the houses he built. After Myrtie's parents (Fultons) died, she inherited home choice properties in Payette. Emet built a new home for them in Payette and one for their daughter, Iris, and her husband, Edward Mordhorst. He acquired a one-room log cabin on the shore of the big Payette Lake at Mc Call, Idaho. It was a minimum facility with no plumbing. Water was pumped and carried from a nearby well. In the late 1930s Emet sold that little cabin and built a large single wall cabin on leased land along the West shore of the Lake. It was big enough to accommodate the family. There was still no plumbing. It had an "outhouse" in back, and water had to be hand pumped and carried up to the kitchen. For those who had to get up in the night there were "slop jars", but everyone slept together in the open loft. It was a great summer get away, with abundant fishing and swimming. Emet enjoyed hunting and fishing even more. He and Myrtie camped out a lot, while fishing for bass and trout. Emet built a camp trailer on a salvaged trailer axel. It was a pretty minimal, but provided shelter and a bed.

Emet hunted and fished to eat. No sportsmanship there, just put it on the table! He always had a fishing pole and tackle in his car, along with an H&R Handygun to get birds wherever he traveled. It was a single shot 410 gauge shotgun with pistol grip and 18 inch barrel.

Emet and Myrtie loved listening to the radio in the evening, for shows like Amos & Andy, George Burns and Gracie Allen, and The Great Gildersleeve. Though Myrtie didn't drink much, Emet enjoyed his evening sips of bourbon and his pipe or a cigar. Though he retired before the Great depression ended, he continued work in carpentry. When the Republicans held the majority of state offices he often managed Payette's state liquor store.

In 1940 through 1944 Emet and Myrtie remodeled the 2 houses on the orchard farms purchased by Leland and Fern Bolt. Myrtie managed the houses and prepared the meals. Their grandson, Leland Emet Bolt, helped with the remodel. Emet had to have a week or two to plan details. After a week, Myrtie would note that no work was being done, but the workers were always there at meal time. The first farm required a new chicken house. The old one had fallen down and the chickens roosted in the trees. They were caught and confined in their new chicken house until they learned it was home. Picture (**305**) shows Myrtie with her chickens on a Bolt fruit farm. Living in those old houses was not easy. There was no plumbing. Water was drawn from a well with the aid of a hand pump and carried into the house. Hot water was heated in a reservoir on the side of an old wood-fired Majestic range. The outhouse was in the rear of the house. Picture (**306**) shows Leland Emet Bolt and the outhouse he built on the first Lee & Fern Bolt farm in the 1940. Picture (316) shows Myrtie about 1941.

*Grandma and her chickens on the Bolt farm.*

*Young Emet Bolt and the "outhouse" he built.*

*Myrtie Brubaker in the 1940s.*

Picture (307) shows the Emet & Myrtie Brubaker Family about 1942.

*Emet, Myrtie and their three daughters.*

Picture (308) shows A. H. Brubaker, his son, Emet, granddaughter, Iris, and great grandson, Dexter about 1946.

*Five generations of Brubakers.*

This was a close family. Iris and her husband, Edward Mordhorst, lived only a block away. Fern and husband lived 30 miles away in Emmett, Idaho.

Hazel and her husband, Charles Collier, lived in western Oregon and Washington, and moved to Emmett in the late 1940s. The families took turns hosting major holiday celebrations. There was always tons of food, and after dinner the kids played in the yard, the women cleaned up and visited, while the men slept!

Myrtie was very resourceful, making toast over an open fire or over flame when the stove lid was removed from the wood-burning stove. Not many products purchased ready-to-eat here. She made everything. They were a great team, dealing with reduced finances or illness and going on to greater achievements. They were able to live at home, with help from their daughters, Hazel, Fern and Iris. Emet died in Payette 4 April 1960, and is buried in Payette's Riverside Cemetery. Myrtie died in the

Emmett, Idaho, hospital in June 1971, and is buried next to her husband in Riverside Cemetery.

Fern Leoline Brubaker married Leland Eddy Bolt 22 May 1924. (see Chapter 3, Leland Eddy Bolt and Fern Leoline Brubaker Family).

Erma Hazel Brubaker married Charles Daly Collier 21 July 1924. Charles was a Civil engineer for the Oregon State Highway Department, and the family moved to many places in western Oregon, wherever his work took them. Picture (309) is a picture of Charles and Hazel about the time they married. They frequently visited Idaho and the Idaho parents and sisters visited in Oregon. Their daughter, Mary Jane Collier, was born 10 November 1932 in Astoria, Oregon, and their son, Charles Michael Collier was born 8 May 1934 in Payette, Idaho. Picture (310) is Mary Jane and Charles Michael Collier with their cousin, Leland Emet Bolt, on a raft on the Sandy river in Oregon.

*Charles and Hazel Collier, soon after their 1924 marriage.*

*Collier and Bolt children on a raft.*

In 1944 things were difficult where the Colliers lived in Portland, Oregon. At the suggestion of Hazel's brother-in-law, Leland Bolt, and her sister, Fern, they came to Emmett, Idaho. They lived on one of Bolt farms and worked in the fruit business.

The farm used German prisoners of war in the harvest season. Ten-year old Charles Michael Collier was terribly afraid of the Germans. But one day a prisoner offered him a Hershey candy bar. Candy was a scarce item back then, so Michael was more relaxed among the prisoners. After the war, Charles again worked as a Civil Engineer, for Morrison & Knudsen Construction Company, at the Hanford Nuclear Reservation in Richland, Washington.

Charles & Hazel's daughter, Mary Jane, worked in the fruit business for several years, rising to packing crew manager. She married Jerry Lee Buck, son of Alvin and Mary Melvina (Hutchins) Buck, 19 May 1951 at Sacred Heart catholic Church in Emmett, Idaho. Jerry went on to become Manager of the Boise Cascade Lumber Mill in Cascade, Idaho. Next, he managed Hampton Lumber Company in Willamina, Oregon. Then the family moved to Sheridan, Oregon, where Jerry and Mary, owned and operated the Reel Buck Market, along with their daughter and son-in-law. Picture (311) shows Mary Jane about 1960.

*Mary Jane (Collier) Buck.*

Jerry established a commercial fishing enterprise in Newport, Oregon. One day in October 1989, while fishing alone from his boat, Jerry disappeared at sea. His boat was found with trailing lines out and food having been prepared on the stove. He was never found. Mary Jane remained in Newport for several years, while working at a local fishing store. She returned to Emmett to be among her high school associates and near her son, Steven.

Their children are:

- JaLinda, born 12 December 1955 in Emmett, married Laurence Lee Lowry 5 July 1975 in Cascade, Idaho. Laurence born 17 April 1953 in Cascade, Idaho.
- Steven Michael Buck born 25 March 1952 in Astoria, Oregon, married Debra Mary Anderson 5 June 1972 in Emmett, Idaho. She was born 15 September 1952 in Emmett, Idaho. She died there 9 November 2005. Their children: Zachariah Freedom Buck (born 24 May 1973), Joshua Alvin Buck (born 28 March 1975), Mary Katherine Buck (born 14 July 1977) and Michael Jacob Buck (born 31 October 1980).

Charles & Hazel's son, Charles Michael Collier, married Barbaranell McMurray 29 December 1959 in Salem, Oregon. Her parents were:

71

Clarence Arthur McMurray, born 23 February 1905 in Walhalla, North Dakota; and Tessa Elaine Weeks, born 20 January 1909 in Leyden, North Dakota. Barbaranell was previously married to an Air Force Officer who died in a training accident in 1956. Their child, Terry Mc Leod, born 14 June 1955 in Mission, Texas, was raised by Charles Michael and Barbaranell.

Charles Michael Collier [see Picture (312)] graduated from University of Idaho, and became an insurance claims adjuster for SAFECO Company. He was drafted into the U. S. Army and served 2 years, then returned to SAFECO. In 1961 he was recalled to Active Army Duty, for the Berlin Crisis. Again released from active duty in 1962, he returned to SAFECO, where he worked a total of 32 years in Salem, Portland and The Dalles, Oregon.

*Charles Michael Collier.*

Their children: Scott Michael Collier, born 26 May 1962 in Madigan Army Hospital, Ft. Lewis (Tacoma) Washington. and Jay Patrick Collier, born 11 October 1968 in The Dalles, Oregon.

Upon graduation from Payette High School in 1929, Iris Eliza Brubaker began working for F. H. Hogue Fruit Company, and became Mr. Hogue's Executive Secretary. She was an outstanding typist and jotted down shorthand notes as fast as anyone could talk. She married Edward Carl Mordhorst 23 July 1934 in Emmett, Idaho. They lived in Payette, but in later years often came to Emmett to help in the seasonal fruit harvests. Iris worked in the F. H. Hogue office. Ed was an expert fruit-picker, and made good money at it. He could pick 400 boxes of apples in a day, and the pay was good. Picture (313) show Iris and Ed about 1948.

*Edward Carl & Iris Eliza (Brubaker) Mordhorst.*

In 1962 Iris became an Assistant Bookkeeper for Emmett Valley Fruits Co., in Emmett, Idaho, until she retired in 1982. She enjoyed many interests, including playing bridge, sewing and knitting. Iris had a wonderful sense of humor, the ability to make activities, stories and accounts funny. She helped write funny broadcasts, which her nephew used in his high school radio announcing competitions. Once, on a hike to a lake near McCall, Idaho, she convinced some Eastern folks that her sister, Fern (black hair in braids) was our Indian guide, and if they did not have such a guide they could be in deep trouble. Humor was so natural with her that she was a wonderful companion and friend that "lifted the spirits" of those with whom she came in contact. Iris and husband, Ed Mordhorst, were long-time residents of Payette, Idaho. When work took them out of town, they stayed with friends or in rented rooms, always returning to Payette

Children of Ed and Iris Mordhorst were: Edward Dexter Mordhorst, born 6 November 1943. and Melanie Jane Mordhorst, born 26 April 1953 in Ontario, Oregon. Edward Dexter Mordhorst married Daryl Berryman 31 August 1974 in Boise, Idaho. Picture (314) is a wedding picture. Their children were: Hallie Kristina Mordhorst, born 30 April 1978 in Boise, Idaho, and Nicholas Edward Mordhorst, born 6 October 1981 in Boise, Idaho. Hallie married (1)

Mathew Duncan 6 July 1997 and their children were Katherine Ann Duncan, born 31 January 1997 in Boise, Idaho, and Luke Mathew Duncan, born 18 November 1999 in Boise, Idaho. Hallie and Mathew Duncan divorced in 2006. She married (2) Jeffery Hetherington 22 August 2009.

*Dexter and Daryl (Berryman) Mordhorst wedding picture.*

Melanie Jane Mordhorst married David Jacob Entzminger 15 October 1977 in Boise, Idaho. He was born in Bitburg, Germany 27 July 1954, while his father was stationed there by the U. S. Air Force. David is a geologist, working for oil companies in west Texas. Picture (315) shows the couple with their children in 1995. Their children are:

- Michael Jacob Entzminger, born 14 April 1980 in Houston, Texas. He married Allison Michelle Curd 25 July 2009 in White Rock, Michigan. Their daughter, Zoe Olivia Entzminger, was born 4 April 2014.
- Joseph David Entzminger, born 8 September 1982 in Aurora, Colorado. He married Sharon Elizabeth Hohlfeld 10 July 2010 in Middletown, Maryland. Their daughter, Emily Catherine Entzminger, was born 3 April 2014.

*David and Melanie (Mordhorst) Entzminger.*

## References:

1. Interview, Myrtie Edna (Fulton) Brubaker, Brubaker & Hill Family Data sheets (Ref. 55)
2. Enclosure to letter, Harlowe Brubaker to Iris Mordhorst April 29, 1965. (Ref. 53)
3. Bolt, Ronald Ben & Martin, Nina Leona; Bolt Americana, Copyright 1968.(Ref. 13)
4. Lordsburg, NM, Grant, Justice of the Peace, Precinct 20, Marriage Certificate 14 June 1903 (Ref. 152)
5. Brubaker - Mordhorst, Iris, "Personal History and Family Record of Emet H. & Myrtie E. Brubaker" 1904 through 1955. (Ref. 189)
6. Certificate of Death, Fern Leoline (Brubaker) Bolt, State of Idaho, Dept. of Health & Welfare, Center for Vital Statistics Instrument Number 2437, page 1 of 1. State File No. 2437, Local Reg. No. 3045
7. Certification of Marriage, Leland E. Bolt & Fern Leoline Brubaker, Clerk of District Court, Payette Co., ID sig. July 20, 1976. (Ref. 41)
8. Obituary, Iris B. Mordhorst, The Idaho Statesman Newspaper, 20 November 1999. (Ref. 127)
9. Bolt, Fern (Brubaker) Bolt, Brubaker Family Notes 1966 (Ref. 57)
10. Mordhorst, Iris (Brubaker), Fulton & Brubaker Family Notes (Ref. 58)

11. Midland, TX, High School Graduation Announcement, Michael J. Entzminger, 23 May 1998 (Ref. 106)
12. Entzminger, Melanie, Letter to Leland Emet Bolt 27 February 1999, Re; their marriage and family data (Ref. 110)
13. Mordhorst, Edward D. Letter to Lee Bolt, Re: his Mordhorst Family data Sheet (Ref. 188)
14. Collier, Michael Letters to Lee Bolt 15 July 2016 and 1 September 2016 (Ref.202)
15. Buck, Mary Jane, Letter to Leland Emet Bolt, re: Collier facts, plus Funeral or Memorial Programs for Jerry Lee Buck, Charles Daly Collier, Mary Melvina Buck and Irma Hazel Collier (Ref 202).

# CHAPTER 3

# Leland and Fern Bolt

# SECTION 1

# The Family

Leland Eddy (Lee) Bolt was drafted into the U. S. Army during World War I. He served about nine months as an infantry Private, but was assigned to care for the large number of Army personnel who got influenza, an epidemic at the time. Picture (400) shows Lee in uniform. Upon discharge from the Army 26 April 1919, he entered Oregon Agricultural College (later Oregon State University) as a Mechanical Engineering student, and joined the Kappa Theta Rho local fraternity (later became Beta Theta Pi). He paid for his Education in many ways. One was raising pigs, which he fed scraps from fraternity & sorority houses. The city put him out of business. No pigs could be raised within city limits. He earned money driving cars from the delivery point in Portland to other cities in Oregon and Washington. He told of driving the Stutz Bearcat, and this was the root of his appreciation for fine automobiles. University life introduced him to dancing and he began smoking cigarettes.

*The Army Private in World War I.*

After more than three years at College, Lee decided that he did not want to be a Mechanical Engineer and quit his studies. His father was extremely disappointed and thought he might be a loser! But, Lee completed a correspondence course in accounting, and got a job with Standard Oil Company. He told of hundreds of girls with comptometers (mechanical calculators) doing the calculations which today are done instantly with computers. He didn't think he was treated well and quit Standard Oil. Returning home to Freewater, Oregon, his father was again concerned. But, Lee took a job with Lamb Fruit Company. His father, Ben, had a long relationship with the Lamb family and their Company. That year (1923) the Milton-Freewater area fruit crops were destroyed by early spring freezes. Lee went to Payette Idaho and found an accounting job with Denny & Company. Picture (401) is Lee in 1923.

*Lee parted his hair in the middle.*

Payette, like most other cities of any size, had at least one public dance hall, where a large part of the population came to dance to the music of big bands. Lee met 17-year-old Fern Leoline Brubaker at the dances. Picture (402) is Fern in 1924. They loved to dance, and Lee met her parents, Emet Hill Brubaker and Myrtie Edna (Fulton) Brubaker, as well as Fern's sister, Hazel. Once or twice a week they enjoyed the dances. Lee took Fern to Milton-Freewater to meet his parents. That turned out well. His grandfather, Chauncey Zimmerman, was also visiting. Chauncey told him; "Young man,

I don't know what this girl sees in you, but you'd better marry her before she changes her mind". As soon as Fern graduated from High School, they were married 24 May 1924 at the home of Reverend Ashworth, Vicar of Payette Episcopal Church. Picture (403) shows Fern as they dressed in 1924. Could be that his mother was relieved, because she had long ago advised him that it was not well for a man to live alone and he should be married by the time he reached 25! He just made it! Picture (404) shows the newlyweds on the steps of the Brubaker home on Center Avenue in Payette.

*Fern at High School graduation.*

*Fern, ready to go to the dance.*

*The newlyweds in 1924*

If Lee's father thought, he had become a nomad; he should have looked further at Fern and the Brubaker family. Fern's parents were real nomads. Perhaps not ranging as far, but this little girl had camped out most of her life. Lee got a job with Denny & Company, owned by Mr. Hogue's son, Denny. He served as a traveling accountant and payments manager for Denny's fruit and vegetable packing and shipping operations. The couple moved to Kent, Washington, and Lewiston, Idaho, where Lee paid the farmers for their crops and kept accounting records. They continued to go to those dances and Lee got in a lot of fishing and hunting, as well. Pictures (405) and (406) show Fern beside their car and wading in the river while Lee fished.

*Fern with the old model T Ford.*

*While Lee fished, Fern went wading.*

In 1928, it was obvious that they would have a child. They returned to Payette, where Lee worked at the F. H. Hogue home office. Picture (407) is their first home on 6th Avenue in Payette. Leland Emet Bolt was born 30 August 1928 at Mrs. Blanchard's home. Dr. Avey was the physician present. Lee gave him the nickname Peewee, because he was Lee or Leland and grandpa Brubaker was known as Emet. In this history with his parents he is Emet, as he was called in school. Fern was a stay at home mom. She and Emet were frequent visitors to friends and the Thurston drug store fountain. They were also close to Fern's sister, Iris, her parents, Emet and Myrtie Brubaker, and the Brubaker great-grandparents, A. H. and Anna Maria (Hill) Brubaker, as well as Emet Brubaker's brother, Scott, and his wife, Genevieve. Scott Brubaker was Manager of Accounting and Sales at F. H. Hogue, Inc. Pictures (408) and (409) show their young son with Lee and Fern. Picture (410) shows the family with Payette friends.

*Lee and Fern's first home.*

*Lee with son, Emet, out in the Payette snow.*

*Fern with Emet, when he was about 2.*

*The family with Payette friends.*

Lee's father-in-law, Emet Brubaker, and Raymond Colton (Emet's brother-in-law) owned and operated an automobile service station on Payette's main street, selling VELTEX products. They also were the Nash automobile dealership. During slow times in the F. H. Hogue office, Lee helped at the service station. Picture (411) shows Lee and his son at the station. Note the tanks on top of the fuel pumps. Fueling began with the tank pumped to the full mark. Following fueling the attendant observed the fuel level and calculated the amount owed.

*Lee and Emet at grandpa's service station.*

Picture (412) shows Fern and her son with her mother and sisters about 1930.

*Emet with his mother, aunts and grandma Brubaker.*

In 1932, Lee was transferred to the F. H. Hogue's Emmett, Idaho, office. Their first home was a tiny little one bedroom apartment in downtown Emmett, next to the train depot. Picture (413) is a 2008 picture of this apartment, which had become a Mexican " hole-in-the-wall" restaurant. Lee could walk less than 200 yards around the Train Depot to the F. H. Hogue office. They had a 1928 Dodge coup, which Fern drove to visit friends in town or at nearby farms.

*That tiny apartment in front of the Chevy pickup*
*had been their first Emmett home.*

The Great Depression was in full force, with very high unemployment and low wages. When Lee reported for work at the F. H. Hogue Emmett office, the Manager had posted a sign on the door, reading "Beginning today the wages at this company are 15 cents per hour. Anyone able to find a higher paying job will be taken to it in my car". One employee got the ride. Lee was fortunate enough to have a salaried bookkeeping job. As businesses failed or cut back, the National Recovery Act was implemented, and Franklin D. Roosevelt became President in 1932. So many had become so desperate, the Government started its own enterprises, like the Civilian Conservation Corps (CCC), Works Progress Administration (WPA) and the Public Works Administration (PWA). Some desperate people got jobs. The Government was in charge, and funded all this by instituting Social Security taxes and higher income taxes. Lee's employer, F. H. Hogue, once took a chance on a venture that could easily have lost $100,000. It turned out well, so he made $100,000 and created short term jobs. But, with the high tax rate (on the rich) at 94%, he got to keep $5,000. He never took such a chance again!

Picture (414) shows the main street of Emmett, Idaho. The city population was about 3,000, but the large farming area made it a thriving small town, particularly on Saturdays, when the farmers came to shop.

*In 1941 Emmett's main street was still about the same as in 1932.*

Lee & Fern moved to a house at 224 Hayes Street at Second Avenue in 1932. Picture (415) is a picture of their second Emmett home. Emet contracted pneumonia in 1933. Without antibiotics, it was a tough recovery. The Catholic Church was in the same block. Father Gallaher visited nearly every day with his jokes and encouragement. The recovery took about 6 months. He had to build his muscles and learn to walk again. Fortunately, Lee & Fern could pay the sizeable Medical bills, including a day nurse. The nurse, Mrs. Shanks, had a pretty daughter, Joanne, about Emet's age. Perhaps Joanne's visits helped motivate recovery, even in a 5-year old boy!

*The Bolt's second Emmett home at corner of Hayes*
*and 2nd Street, as it was in 2008.*

Lee fished and hunted every season and brought game for the dinner table. When hunting, he carried Emet on his shoulders. When the dog set a bird, he'd lower Emet to ground and command the dog to get the bird into the air. He'd shoot the bird and the dog retrieved it. The bird was secured in his vest and Emet boosted to his shoulders and the hunt continued.

About 1934 the WPA was doing a trenching job across Hayes Street from their house. The supervisor was George Knowles, the local surveyor. He enjoyed Emet's visits. But, once when he left he told Emet he should take his place. When he returned, Emet reported who leaned on their shovel or visited and did little work!

Fern and Lee still went to the week-end dances to the big bands. It wasn't Glen Miller or the Dorsey brothers, but the part-time musicians did a great job. Lee & Fern rarely got a baby sitter. While at the dances, they "parked" Emet with the trombonist, Oliver Fry.

On the short walk home from the F. H. Hogue office, Lee often stopped by the butcher shop and bought meat for dinner. The package was taken by their dog (Sport), who ran on ahead. Upon reaching the house he put the package at the door and barked. Alerted by the dog, Fern put the main course on to cook, and Sport got a small reward too!

It was a great depression era, but the Brubaker families were very frugal, exchanging or passing down items of fashion and furniture. They made many items, like the Picture (416) hooked rug, made from strips of used fabric. This is a smaller example, but larger (e. g. 5' x 8') rugs graced the floors of larger rooms.

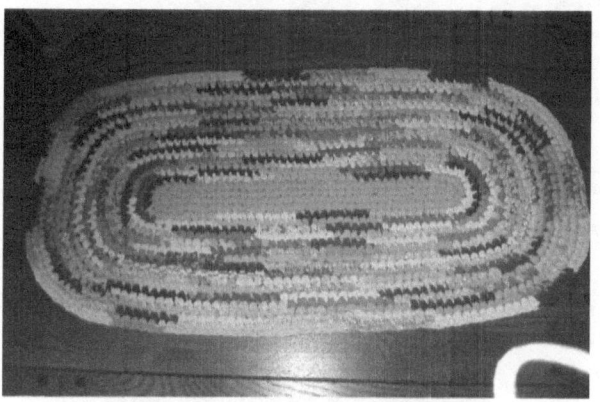

*The Brubaker families made many household*
*items, like this rug, from scrap fabrics.*

About 1934 the family moved to a home at 703 North Washington Street. The area was called Mill Town, because the local Weyerhaeuser Lumber Company built the original homes for the employees. Picture (417) is a 2008 picture of their home, and Picture (418) shows Emet in the yard. This residence rented for $30 per month, and they found a place 3 blocks away at 421 Commercial Street for $25. Picture (419) is this home, and Lee still had a short distance of the office. They rented a room to help pay the rent, but that didn't go well, with either the girl first, then a man. Lee found another source of income when a Fruit Drying company in near-by Fruitland was found to be bankrupt and its books "cooked". Lee and Ken Nash (from Hogue's Payette office) earned extra money reconstructing the books and assisting in the bankruptcy process. Lee also earned extra money as a movie theater attendance checker, for movies which theater cost were based upon attendance. He'd report to those theaters with a counter in his pocket and take the official attendance. Results were reported to the theater and movie distributor. Fern and Emet often accompanied him, and were admitted free. They told of seeing Alexander's Ragtime Band six times.

*The third Emmett home was near the Payette river bridge on Washington Street.*

*On Washington Street the family had a back yard for the first time.*

*The 4th Emmett home was in in Mill Town, 4 blocks from Lee's office.*

In 1936 Fern began working for Dr. C. B. Titus, a local dentist. With no formal schooling, she was trained on the job. To make children's visits more enjoyable, she cast figures in Plaster of Paris, like Snow White and the seven dwarfs. Sometimes she painted them. Picture (420) shows the family photo of the year. With both parents working, whenever Emet was out of school he had to keep one of the parents informed of his whereabouts. This was the 1930s, so he picked up the phone and Flossy, the operator, asked "number please?" Emet replied "46", and Flossy connected him with the F. H. Hogue office. It was reported that Flossy knew more than anyone about what was "going on" in the Emmett area.

*Lee & Fern Bolt family about 1938.*

Emet earned money substituting on paper routes and shining shoes. Gamage's barber shop had 5 chairs and a bath in the back for use by people passing through. The shoeshine boy had to clean the tub and lay out towels & soap for the bathers, then cleanup for the next customer. They were mostly cowboys and sheepherders, who really needed cleaning up!

In 1938 Lee was promoted to Manager of the F. H. Hogue Emmett Operations, which included the fruit packing operation and three 40-acre fruit farms. Picture (421) shows Lee at work in the office. In the rear is the stand-up desk he worked at in his bookkeeper days. All transactions were entered in a Journal, from which each entry was posted (by hand) into each ledger account at month end. The sum for each Ledger account was manually entered in the Balance Sheet, and all the debits had to equal the credits – exactly! Lee often worked for hours to find every error, no matter how small. What a difference computers have made!

*Lee, smoking away, while typing, at the F. H. Hogue office.*

Soon after becoming the F. H. Hogue Emmett Manager, Lee was up on the back porch mixing spray materials. Young John Bohlin came by and asked if he could get a job. Lee hired him to do what he'd been doing. John became the chief engineer, automating packing processes and solving problems. He was Lee's "right-hand man" and friend for the rest of his business career. In the late 1930s an Obermeyer boy died of Rocky Mountain spotted fever, a blood-to-blood transmitted disease, usually by ticks. Emmett instituted a vaccination program that required a shot in both arms on 3 different days. The Bolts and John Bohlin got their shots from Hazel, a nurse at the Mary Secor County Hospital. John said she saved the dull and bent needles for use on him. John married Hazel, and they had a boy, Brent, and a girl, Brenda.

Mr. Hogue told Lee it was time to buy his own farm. He found the Lemmer farm, and F. H. said "buy it"! After some discussion about Lee having no down payment, Mr. Hogue got him a loan from Mrs. Hogue. That 25-acre farm was about 15 miles southwest of town, with prune trees, a small grape vineyard and a corn field. It was the right time buy. Lee & Fern paid for it with the crops harvested the first year. Eventually, Italian prune and peach trees covered the whole farm. The house had two bedrooms with no bathroom or plumbing. Water was drawn from a hand pump in the back yard, and there was an "outhouse" as well. Fern's father and mother, Emet and Myrtie Brubaker, moved to the farm to make the house more livable, build a new chicken house and repair the barn. New floors were installed in the house. A new "outhouse" was built and the old wood-fired range cleaned and updated. Young Emet lived with them when school was not in session, and helped grandpa. Picture (422) shows the farm after more orchards were planted.

*The Bolts first orchards were 25 acres on the Emmett Valley South slope.*

A few years later Lee bought another 25 acre farm in the same area. See Picture (423). With that purchase Lee & Fern's farms covered about 65 acres, because about 15 acres was between the irrigation canal and the second Bolt farm that could not be accessed by anybody else. State statute ruled that such isolated pieces of property may be used by the adjacent property owner(s). Emet & Myrtie Brubaker and their grandson, Emet, moved in during the summer and updated the house. Again, no inside plumbing and an outside privy.

*The second Bolt orchards were near the first.*

Not only had the Government taken on jobs usually done by the private sector, they passed out money to advance their issues and ideas. For example, in 1939 a man from the U. S. Bureau of Reclamation presented Lee a check for $3,000. He said it was for growing alfalfa, which inhibited erosion in his fruit orchards. That was more than Lee's annual salary! But, he hadn't had a good day until then, and this Government "handout" infuriated him. He advised the man that they grew alfalfa to crowd out the sandburs that otherwise caused terrible grief for fruit-pickers. He ordered the man to take the check and get out of his office, and rounded the end of the counter after him. When the man quickly departed, Lee turned and said "That guy could have mashed me". The guy was a lot bigger. Lee said people are generally reluctant to take on anyone that angry.

There were homeless persons, mostly hobos who rode trains from coast to coast. They generally lived by the railroad car storage areas and sometimes came to our door to ask if they could work for food. We'd find something they could do. In the summer, there was plenty of work in the farm industry, so conditions improved. But, in the northwest the winters were devastating. Emmett was a mill town, and workers' families were regimented to their work schedule. Fathers reported for work at 7:00 AM and most took half a can of sinews (Copenhagen) as they clocked in. At noon, they ate lunch (brought from home) and took the other half can of Copenhagen. At 5:00 PM they got off work and at 5:30 dinner was served at all mill worker homes. All play ceased, and the kids were at the table.

Idaho became home to lots of Basque families from their home area of Northern Spain. They had been loyal to the Spanish King Alphonso, and fled to this country during the Franco revolution. They were mainly lumber mill workers and sheepherders. Emmett had a large sawmill and was home to the Andrew Little Sheep Company (one of the world's largest). It was ideal for the Basque immigrants. Emet had many friends to play with in Mill Town. They got together a softball team and arranged games with the only other city area able to field a team, Williams Addition. The games were stressful, because the teams provided the referees. Disputes were common. But, one of Emet's best friends was Joe Garatea, a Basque Williams Addition player. He was often at Joe's house and ate there, or Joe ate at the Bolt home. Joe's father had died in a mill accident years before they met. They remained close friends during their school years.

Lee had trouble keeping a bookkeeper and Office Manager. Girls were hired, but once they learned the bookkeeping job they would find a husband and/or leave town. Despite cautions against man and wife working closely together, Fern became the F. H. Hogue Office Manager and Bookkeeper. In harvest season, Fern's sister, Iris, and husband, Ed, came to Emmett to help, Iris in the office and Ed was a superior fruit picker. Picture (424) shows Fern and Iris working in the office. Picture (425) shows Lee and Fern with the packing house crew supervisor.

*Iris came to assist in the F. H. Hogue office at harvest time.*

*Mrs. Wills, packing crew supervisor, with Lee & Fern in front of*
*the board of fruit labels used in F. H. Hogue packaging.*

In 1940 Fern's father, Emet Brubaker, built Lee and Fern a new home
at 411 W. Second Street. Picture (426) shows the house in a 2008
picture. It had a half basement, two bedrooms, one bath, kitchen and
dining room. When the basement and subfloor were complete, Emet
asked Fern and Lee to come and express their desires on the planned
rooms. Fern had several ideas, that her father declared could not be
accommodated. It turned out that the house could only be the same as
the homes he had built for himself and for Fern's sister, Iris. He only
built one floor plan. The Larsens lived next door, with their 3 sons
and a daughter. Lawrence Larsen, though a year older, became Emet's
close friend in High School. Emet made a basketball backboard from
tongue & groove flooring, affixed a rim and net. It was attached to the
rear of the garage. That alley basketball court attracted many players,
though the dirt alley was a very uneven surface for dribbling the ball.
Winter was worse!

*A 2008 picture of the home Fern's father built on Second Street.*

When in the 7th grade, one of Emet's friends had a birthday party in which attendees must come with a date. He was not very interested in going, but friends suggested Avonne Wilcox would go with him, and they'd cleared the way for him to ask her. She accepted, and the date was on. Emet told his Dad, who asked when he was to pick her up? Their plans to meet at a church along the way were not well received. Lee said "when you have a date you go pick her up and take her the party. Further, you go in and meet her father". Emet said "Meet her father?" Lee said; "yes, I will take you to her house at the proper time. You will go in and meet her father, and then I'll drive you to the party and we'll see that she is returned to her home". It was a good party, and Avonne became a good friend.

On December 7, 1941 Emet and his friends were playing basketball in the alley behind the 2nd street home. Lee brought news of the Japanese attack on Pearl Harbor and the Hawaiian island of Oahu. Not knowing much about the situation the boys said "They'll regret that" and went on with the game. The United States entered World War II, and soon some of those basketball players were in the Armed Services. Yes, the Japanese did eventually regret it, but Germany entered the war and we were defending on both the Atlantic and Pacific. The Japanese won battle after battle. Over the next 4 years the United States slowly turned the tide.

Until we entered the war, there were many organized Nazi sympathizers, who had "black shirt" youth groups in larger metropolitan areas (e.g. New York & Los Angeles). Adolph Hitler was a hero to some. There was also Gus Hall and a sizeable active Communist party.

High unemployment and business failures had continued through the 1930s, though some progress was made. What really brought this country out of the desperate times was World War II. It was then that the Government challenged private industry to create the industrial might that was needed to win a war that was bigger than any before. This United States industrial might was what the Japanese Admiral Yamamoto had warned the Imperial Japanese Military about before the Pearl Harbor attack. Private industry was converted overnight. Vacuum cleaner plants were making machine guns, auto plants produced tanks and aircraft engines. In rapid response, automobile manufacturers were producing tanks and combat vehicles. Ships were being built in a few months, and new aircraft were catching up with the Japanese and Germans. The result was that our capability rapidly developed to supply our forces and allied forces to win against formidable enemies in Asia and Europe.

Although it was the men of the United States armed forces who did the fighting and the dying, America's home front worked miracles toward final victory. It was that white flame of total war that truly fused this whole nation together. Unique and massive financing (by the American taxpayer), huge production of armaments, and the ability to move this equipment abroad with dispatch finally overpowered the Axis powers. America was still the land of muscle (which the enemy mistakenly thought had become flabby) and American know-how turned the tide. In 1939, two percent of our gross national product was armaments. By 1942, it quadrupled; by 1944 the United States assembly lines were generating fifty percent more war materials than the *total* enemy output.

In 1942 the government prohibited people of Japanese descent (citizens or not) living within 200 miles of our coast. Those unable to relocate were housed at inland area camps. One such camp was in Tule Lake, California. One of the Japanese interned there, Herb Tanoye, called Lee and said he did not want his family to experience that camp. He said if they could get employment outside the restricted coastal area, they could live and work there. Lee hired Herb, and many more. These laborers were critical to the fruit packing industry in growing, harvesting and shipping hundreds of railroad cars of fresh fruit every year. For the next four years, these people worked and lived in Emmett. Herb, his wife, May, and son, Eddie, lived on Lee's Ranch for a time. Herb became the manager of the displaced Japanese employees, and later foreman for all workers at Lee's ranch and the F. H. Hogue ranches.

Mr. Wilcox, the father of Avonne (Emet's friend and first date in 1938) was a buyer for the Golden Rule Stores. He had acquired a lot and built a magnificent home at the head of Evergreen Drive, a long oval drive off East Main Street. It was built by Hubert Martin, one of Idaho's very best builders. Picture (427) is a 2008 picture of the home. In 1942 Mr. Wilcox was drafted and the family left town until after the war. Lee & Fern bought their home. Emet thought living there would make friends look upon him as a rich kid and alienate them. In fact, it was just the opposite. He had more friends.

*In 1942 the Bolts bought one of the best homes in Emmett.*

With Lee and Fern both working, help was needed at home. Herb helped Lee find a suitable home assistant. The first candidate was a Buddhist girl of Japanese ancestry, whose family had done very well prior to the war. She had a little Buddhist alter in her room. Lee's mother, the good Baptist, came to visit and saw an opportunity to make a convert! That didn't work out well. Herb then found Harriet, the wife of Frank Mihara. He was one of the workers of Japanese descent in the F. H Hogue work force. Harriet had grown up in Seattle and was a wonderful choice. She managed the home and learned to cook like Fern. She was like a second mother to Emet and his cousin, Dexter Mordhorst, who came with his parents at harvest time. She was a Baptist, so there was no problem with grandma Bolt. Picture (428) is a picture of Harriet at the time.

*Harriet was a wonderful addition to the Bolt Family.*

In 1942 and 43 Lee had his second farm planted with apples and pears. Mr. Hogue bought the Model Fruit Farm and his son bought another 40 acre farm on the valley's South slope. Emet and his friend, Lawrence Larson, precisely staked out the tree locations and then helped dig the planting holes at all three farms. Lee now managed five 40 acre Hogue fruit farms, plus his own 65 acres. In further support of the war effort the company grew potatoes on leased land west of town, near the Uncle Tom's Cabin junction.

By 1944, three and one-half million "Rosie, the Riveters" and six million men turned out cargo ships and planes in record times. People bought forty-nine billion dollars in War Bonds. We grew our own food in Victory Gardens, even though farmers were producing enough food to feed half a world and their armies.

Civil Defense Corps volunteers were identifying and reporting planes and ships. Even tiny Emmett, Idaho, had air raid drills. Emet was an emergency messenger, who reported on his bicycle to the Idaho Power Company office. In case of communication disruption, he was to carry the messages to outlying places. Others made carefully crafted models of world aircraft, as training aids for spotters. These models had to precisely meet drawings and specifications.

Kids saved empty toothpaste tubes and all true-blue Americans turned into attic and basement scavengers, collecting used metal. There was massive salvaging of everything from old pots and pans to flattened-out used food cans.

Citizens received books of ration stamps in various colors for gasoline, cigarettes, meat, sugar, etc. Yet, ironically, Americans ate *more* food and spent more money on these items than at any other time previously.

As key import sources were no longer possible, our country made scientific discoveries for war. We developed Radar, flame throwers, rocket launchers, jet engines, and many other lethal weapons of war. Sulfa drugs, Penicillin and successive antibiotics were discovered to cure previously incurable diseases; DDT to fight jungle insects came home after the war. The use of blood plasma instead of whole blood gave life to multitudes. Rayon and nylon substituted for silk.

Though Lee was in his early 40s and manager of a fruit growing and processing operation, it was possible he could be drafted into the armed forces. Lee, Fern and Emet had a future planning session at their farm, to make decisions about what to do if Lee went back to the Army. Fortunately, food production was a big priority too, so Lee stayed to help institute new food processing in support of the war effort.

The industrial might of this country resulted in not only winning the war, but evolving the world's most prosperous economy, with inventiveness and personal freedoms the envy of the world. Instead of imposing war reparations on Germany and Japan, as was done to Germany after World War I, the United States implemented programs (like the Marshall Plan) to rebuild former enemy nations and economies.

Emet and his friends were usually playing sports. It may have begun with the softball teams, but continued into high school. Emet joined his friends in trying out for the eighth grade and high school teams. He was barely 5 foot 6 inches and weighed about 125 lbs. The football coach said, "Emet you can be a guard". So, he was looking across the line at farm kids twice his size. Basketball was big in Emmett. Emet turned out for it with his friends, who were usually over 6 foot tall. He did play a lot of basketball on varsity teams, because he learned to bring the ball down the floor against anyone, and get it in to the guys that could score. These high school athletics took place during World War II, when resources were rationed. Lee was in the business of producing food, so had a nearly unlimited ration of gasoline. Many times, he saved the day by getting Emmett High School teams to games in nearby cities.

The Payette River froze in winter, and the boys played hockey on the ice. Two rocks about 8 feet apart were the goals at each end of the playing area. Hockey sticks were cut tree or bush limbs, preferably with a knot on the end. The pucks were tin cans beat into round shapes. As games proceeded the pucks got more lethal for the players. There were no referees. The boys settled their own disputes.

Fern (with Lee's help), the Nolands and Smokes started the Black Canyon Riders horse & saddle club. They performed drills (e.g. horsemanship & barrel races) at rodeos and fairs at nearby towns. Picture (429) shows a saddle club breakfast and coyote hunt. They built the bleachers at the Gem County Fair Grounds in Emmett. The Bolts had three horses; Pard, a gaited show horse, who loved parades; Rex, a pinto trained to do a few tricks; and Patsy, a feisty little mare. Lee, Emet and friends rode the horses on long trips into the Idaho primitive areas. The excuse was fishing, and they did fish (trout and salmon). But, the main "drawing card" was the trip itself. Two of Lee's cowboy friends, Ray Bentley & Don Shoemaker, were experienced travelers in these remote areas. They alternated as guides. Trips took a week or more, in which the riders encountered bear, deer, elk, rattlesnakes, porcupines and other wild life. Emet's cousins, Don Denman & Ben Bolt, and his friend, Don Buck, often were among the travelers. Picture (430) shows Emet and Don Buck on one of the pack trips. The guides arranged for the pack mules to carry food and equipment, and extra horses as necessary. They took turns showing the remote areas, and playing jokes on the teenagers. Once on a short trip to a lake near Mc Call, Idaho, Fern's sister, Iris, husband, Ed, Lee, and Emet were walking. Fern was riding Pard. She had dark black hair in two braids. Her complexion was tanned, so she resembled a Native American. Upon encountering a group that was obviously foreign to the area, Iris asked who their guide was. She implied that Fern was our Indian guide and everyone needed a guide. Fern was stoic and quiet. So, we had some fun too. Picture (431) shows Harry Lyons, Lee, and Emet as they returned to the Bolt cabin at McCall to Join Fern, Ruth Lyons and the two Lyons daughters (Ilene and Clarice) for a post-trip celebration. This was the first cabin Lee and Fern owned on the Payette Lakes at Mc Call, Idaho. It was built on leased land by Fern's father, Emet Brubaker, from whom they bought it. Lee said Emet stayed in it more after he sold it than when he had owned it. It was a summer cabin of single wall construction. The "out house" was in the rear and water was hand pumped from the well out front. There was no beach, but it had that big front porch with a wonderful view of the lake. The kitchen and living space was all downstairs and everyone slept in the open 2$^{nd}$ floor. Fern went there once in the winter, with Emet and several of his friends. They heated with available wood, and cooked meals on a small wood-fired stove. The memory of such ravenous and constant appetites ensured Fern wouldn't do it in winter again. But, with the demands of farm work in summer, a few days on the lake were like heaven on earth.

*The Black Canyon Riders became an exciting saddle club.*

*Emet and his friend, Don Buck, wrestled with a salmon.*

*Bolts, Lyons and Don Buck at the Mc Call cabin.*

Emet learned to be a farmer and did every job in the fruit packing facility and trucking fruit and supplies. For farm work, Lee would come to his bedroom about 4:30AM and say "Pop out now. You need to get to work". Emet hoped he'd go away, but he didn't. After another wake-up call, he'd give his speech: "I don't care if you ever work another day of your life, you will learn how now! Pop out and get going!" That would do it until the next time. Emet was at work by 6:00 AM. In the harvest season, there was always extra work. Once Emet was working a full shift at the packinghouse, then loading a truck with containers and driving to supply a packer in a nearby town. At other times, he hauled 100lb sacks of sugar from the Caldwell, Idaho, sugar beet factory, for use in preparing frozen pie cherries. In those days, there were no bins and forklifts. Every box of fruit had to be individually loaded and unloaded.

In Emmett, High School basketball was king. The team won the Idaho state championship in 1942, when there were no different competitions based upon size of student body. Emmett had to beat schools like Boise, which had 10 times as many players from which to choose. Emmett High School had been playing in the Methodist Church recreation hall, but a new high school Gymnasium was built. The games were always well attended, and there was unusual talent. The 1944 and 1945 basketball teams placed second in the state championship tournament. Emet managed to play on the 1945 and 1946 teams. He also played on the 1946 tennis team. Having earned his letter, he was initiated into the E club in 1945. The initiation included having the entire E club give him spats with paddles. About that time, the cute daughter of the nurse who attended him during his 1933 bout with pneumonia had come to town and Emet had a date with her. After the rear-end beating, it was not the greatest time to date a pretty girl.

Emet's neighbor and high school friend, Lawrence Larsen, was a two year All State Basketball player. Picture (432) shows Lawrence and Emet in 1945. After College, Lawrence was drafted by the Philadelphia 76ers NBA team.

*Emet wth his friend and 2ⁿᵈ street neighbor, Lawrence Larson.*

As a senior in High School, Emet joined the public speaking and debate team, in the Radio Announcing category. His aunt, Iris, was great help in devising funny programs. In one, Emet was the announcer for a basketball game between two area rivals. School and player names were thinly disguised. The game was between Coldwall (really Caldwell) and Campa (really Nampa). The big guy for Coldwall was Tim Scramond (really Jim Hamond) and the other four players Ole Gaggan, Billy

Karush, Bill Piff and Joe Jones. For Campa, it was Ben Bushman (really Cushman), Smith, Smith, Smith and Kirkenschlager. One action under the basket, going for the rebound, the announcer (Lee) says "Tim Scramond throws an elbow at Bushman, who retaliates with a lefty hook to the jaw, all unnoticed by referee Tattle (Real name Tuttle), who seems to be waiving at someone in the audience!" This and similar scripts enabled Emet to win the southwestern Idaho radio announcing championship. But the state championship rules required a historical story. He chose the story of Chief Joseph, the notorious Nez Perce Indian chief, and came in second.

Lee and Fern helped Emet prepare for High School events, like the Graduation Banquet, for which he was the Master of Ceremonies. And they helped him find clothing and articles to be Josef Stalin at the Masquerade Ball. Picture (433) shows Stalin and some of the other attendees. High School graduation was a big event in Emmett, a town of about 3,000 residents. Picture (434) shows Emet's graduation picture.

*Don Buck, Pat Adams, Don Reynolds, Betheen Mc Neelly*
*and Emet at the high school Masquerade Ball.*

*Emet at high school graduation.*

In 1945 Lee was asked to run for Emmett City Council, which he did, and was elected. This began his long terms of service to the city of Emmett. in city government.

Emet never lost his desire to go to the U. S. Naval Academy and become a Naval Officer, although he probably didn't fully understand the career path he was seeking. Lee and Fern desired that he come to Emmett and eventually run the business, but they supported him in his desire for a Navy career. Lee had to find out what was required, and visited several Congressmen and a Senator. In 1947, Emet got a 1st Alternate Senatorial Appointment, plus 2nd and 3rd Alternates from Congressmen. With no councilors on the school staff, Emet missed taking chemistry and had not done well in Physics. Lee sent him to Rutherford School, a preparatory school in Long Beach California. Without that additional instruction, he may not have had a Navy career.

With Emet away to Rutherford School in February 1947, Lee & Fern traveled in winter to see the Southwest and visit him. Picture (435) is Lee & Margaret and Walter Smoke in front of the Los Angeles Conservatory. Picture (436) is Lee and Fern in front of their hotel in Wickenburg, Arizona. They were in Yuma, Arizona, 20 February. Fern's notes say they went to Mexicali, and dined at a Chinese restaurant in Calexico. She commented about how the authorities checked their possessions at the borders of California, Arizona and Mexico. Then they went on to Long Beach, California, where they saw Emet. They took him, and fellow students Jack Cromwell and John Allen to Earl Carrol's Vanities, a prominent Hollywood night club. Picture (437) is the Club souvenir poster. The bill was $94! Then they went on to San Francisco, and then to Medford, Oregon, where Ken Denman, Walter and Lee went fishing. Then, it was on home through Portland, Oregon. Fern wrote that it was a trip they'd never forget.

*Lee with Walter & Margaret Smoke, traveling in Arizona.*

*Fern & Lee in Wickenburg, Arizona.*

*The famous Earl Carrol Nightclub brochure.*

Rutherford School was at 1250 East Ocean Blvd in Long Beach, with 100 yards of sandy beach to the shore. Picture (438) is Emet and John Allen at the beach volleyball net.

*Students played volleyball on the sandy beach behind Rutherford School dormitory.*

Emet completed the Rutherford School program and the USNA entrance examinations in the spring of 1947. Upon returning home he was notified that Senator Taylor's Principal appointee refused the appointment. That meant Emet would be appointed if he passed the entrance examinations. While awaiting examination results, Lee put him to work. A week or so later Lee drove out to the farm where Emet was loading fruit, with news that he passed . Emet was ecstatic, and said he was quitting, but Lee said "no, you must complete this job"!

In June 1947 Emet flew to the nation's capital. Lee's uncle Ottamar Hamele, husband of Lee's deceased aunt, Mattie (Zimmerman) Hamele, was a Federal Attorney in Washington D. C. He had done much for the family. He met Emet, and showed him around the Capital. Then it was on to Annapolis, where he was sworn in 13 June 1947 as Midshipman 4th Class Leland Emet Bolt, USN. All his clothing and possessions were packed in a box and sent home, where his mother opened it and shed tears. The new Midshipmen were given the uniforms and other items to begin their first year of training.

Lee & Fern had an empty nest, but plenty of work. In winter the orchards were dormant and little work required. Except for that trip with the Smokes to the southwest and Mexico, they had never been far out of the Northwest. In July of 1947. Fern managed to take her sister, Iris and her son, Dexter, up to their cabin at McCall. It was a great break from the heat and workload in Emmett. Pictures (439) and (440) show Fern and Harriet in the lake, and Harriet and Dexter on a stump.

*Fern and Harriet in the Payette Lake at Mc Call, Idaho.*

*Harriet closely watched Dexter at the Payette Lake.*

After 1947 they drove several times through the Midwest and South, visiting their son in Annapolis. Of course, Fern always loved entertaining her friends and Family. Picture (441) shows a birthday party Fern hosted for a friend.

*Fern lived to give parties, like on Marie Rude's Birthday.*

Lee was an active member of the Northwest Fruit and Vegetable Association (now Oregon Idaho Fruit and Vegetable Assn.) and served a term as a Director. The first order of business at each meeting was to affirm objection to Federal farm subsidies. Their position was that subsidies encouraged the inefficient and promoted big conglomerates that "gamed the system" for profit. He served a term as President of the Idaho state Horticultural Society. Governor Samuelson appointed him to the District Magistrates Commission of Judicial District No. 3.

Lee and Fern had plenty to keep them busy, with the F. H. Hogue business growing and Lee getting huge city projects accomplished. They still participated in the Black Canyon Riders Club and the Gem County Rodeo. Lee signed up the contestant cowboys and was the Rodeo Secretary. Picture (442) is Lee and the Rodeo Clown. Until about 1948 their travels were limited to fishing and hunting trips and visiting relatives in the Northwest. Then, with Emet off to the Naval Academy, they began traveling to the Eastern seaboard and South.

*Lee and the clown at the Gem County Fair.*

Lee and Fern rented a house in Annapolis for their son's gradation June 1, 1951. Lee took 8mm films of the graduation activities and ceremonies. Jacqueline Joyce Barker, their son's fiancé, and Uncle Ottamar came. Uncle Ottamar told the new Ensign: "Young man, your lady friend is very pleasing of face and figure". After the presentation of diplomas and throwing their Midshipman caps in the air, their son became Ensign Leland Emet Bolt, USN. His orders were to report to San Diego, California, for Amphibious Warfare School, then report aboard USS LENAWEE (APA-195). The new Ensign and Miss Barker took the train to New York City, where they stayed at the Roosevelt Hotel and saw a couple of Broadway shows. Jacqueline returned to her job at the Naval War College in Newport, Rhode Island, and Ensign Bolt flew to Chicago, where he met his parents and drove them back to Emmett. They stopped in Red Oak, Iowa, where Lee was born and found the shoe store his father had sold about 1906 was still in business with the same name, Bolt shoe Company. Picture (443) shows the shoe store in 1951.

*The Bolt Shoe Company was in business in 1951,*
*long after Lee's dad sold it in 1906.*

Ensign Bolt completed Amphibious warfare School in San Diego, California, and proceeded on to LENAWEE. In September he reported aboard LENAWEE in Sasebo, Japan, where it was deployed in support of the Korean war. Upon the ship's return to San Diego in late 1951, Jacqueline Barker came to San Diego and found employment. Ensign

Bolt and Miss Barker were married June 15, 1952 at St. Marys Church in Emmett, by the Episcopal Bishop of Idaho, Frank A. Rhea. Picture (444) is the wedding party. The Best Man (Ensign Donald D. Buck USN) and Matron of Honor (Shirley Thurman) are on the left and Ushers (ENS Francis J. Degnan and ENS D. Wisdom USN of Boise) on the right. Jacqueline's family was unable to attend. Emet's uncle, Kenneth G. Denman, gave the bride away. The reception was hosted by Lee & Fern's neighbors, the Calendars. Family friends, Robert & Jesse Naylor, gave the newlyweds the Bridal Suite at the Hotel Boise. The newlyweds went on to Sun Valley resort, then up over the mountains through Stanley to Warm Lake and the Bolt cabin at Mc Call. Upon arrival back in Emmett, the Smokes, Naylors and many more seized the newlyweds and made them each push the other in a wheelbarrow over five blocks of Main Street. Escapes didn't work, and the leaders decreed that if the couple could not come up with strong drink, he would go to Pearl (a mountain community to the North) and she to Fruitland, a town to the South. Remembering a left-over battle of champagne, ENS Bolt told them he could provide the "booze". They returned to the Bolt home, where the groom poured each one a shot glass of champagne. They could not argue, because they had not said how much!

*The newly-weds and the wedding party.*

Lee had been serving on the Emmett City Council, and in 1953 he was encouraged to run for Mayor. He was elected and served 6 years. He had seen the state of the city and Government processes, so knew the challenges of managing city affairs as well as F. H. Hogue operations. Fern was a big contributor to the city management. She loved entertaining, and big crowds the best. She had plenty of impressive sets of dishes and silverware. No paper plates and plastic here! A cooking assistant helped prepare the food and set the tables. Fern managed the operation as a professional. The annual Cherry Festival and visiting Mayors could depend upon great food and service.

Fern and Lee began "wintering" in Southern California cities and towns, like Indio and San Diego, where they visited their son and Jacqueline. By April of 1954 they had two grandsons, Leland Emet Bolt Jr and Jon Warner Bolt. Before long the grandsons were spending some summer days with their grandparents in Idaho. When they were old enough, Lee put them to work on his farms. In 1959 a third grandson, Stuart Clay Bolt, was born in San Diego. So, now three boys came to work for grandpa. But, there were fun times too, like riding in the Cherry Festival Parade with the Mayor and the city's First Lady. And they got to go to Mc Call on the Payette Lake, where Lee and Fern had a summer house.

Lee completed his first terms as Mayor in 1959, but lost election for City Council 3$^{rd}$ ward. It was probably a good thing, because in 1962, Mr. Hogue died and the heirs assigned a family member to manage their Emmett operations. It was just what was needed to motivate Lee to start his own Fruit Packing Company. He selected partners and started Emmett Valley Fruits. The partners were John Bohlin, his longtime Chief Engineer he hired for F. H. Hogue Company, and Ernie Radke, an owner of stores. Ernie moved right into the sales end of the business. They leased buildings near a railroad spur and convenient for truck loading and offload.

By 1964 Emmett Valley Fruits was doing over $3 million in gross sales and growing every year. A new packing, cold storage and office building was added for the growing business.

Lee & Fern loved their grandchildren, and they came in summer to work on the farm. Picture (449) shows Lee & Fern with their son and daughter-in-law, Jacqueline, and the 3 boys, Leland Emet Bolt jr., Jon Warner Bolt and Stuart Clay Bolt.

*Lee & Fern with grandsons and their parents.*

Lee was elected Mayor again, taking office in January 1964. He served another 8 years, while managing Emmett Valley Fruits and traveling in winter.

Their summer home in Mc Call, Idaho, was a great get-away and they used it more often. Pictures (450) and (451) show the "cabin" exterior and living area. It's the cabin John Bohlin built for them in the late 1940s. It was a summer only house, a hundred yards from the Payette Lake shore. Oh, yes. It had plumbing and bathrooms!

*The Bolt summer cabin was near the big Payette Lake.*

*Lee and Emet in the cabin at Mc Call.*

With all the pressing obligations, Lee and Fern had a wonderful love of the parties and fun events. Picture (453) shows the witch and "lady of the night" with their son at a 1986 San Diego Halloween party.

*Lee and Fern enjoyed having fun times too.*

The Idaho Statesman was Idaho's primary daily newspaper and published in Boise. The paper designated Lee as 1972 Distinguished Citizen. Picture (454) is the newspaper artist's sketch. The news article recognized him for:

- Service on the Emmett City Council and as Mayor.
- 25 years as manager of F. H. Hogue Company Emmett operations, including commercial fruit packing and shipment, and managing several hundred acres of fruit orchards.
- Starting in Emmett Valley Fruits in 1962
- 32nd degree Mason Membership in Boise's El Korah Shrine.
- Past President of the Idaho State Horticultural Society.
- Selected "Man of the Year" by Emmett Jaycees in 1965.
- Governor Don Samuelson appointed him to the District Magistrate's Commission of Judicial District No. 3
- Service as a Director of the Idaho Oregon Fruit and Vegetable Association.
- Many years as Secretary of the Gem County Rodeo Committee.
- American Legion Member

*The Idaho Statesman artist's sketch of the Distinguished Citizen.*

Picture (455) is Lee and Fern at their 50th wedding anniversary party, with their son, daughter-in-law and three grandsons; Leland Emet Bolt jr., Jon Warner Bolt, and Stuart Clay Bolt.

*Everyone in Lee & Fern's family was present for their*
*50th Wedding Anniversary in 1974*

About 1979 John Bohlin and Ernie Radke chose to sell their partnership shares. John stayed on as Chief Engineer, and Ernie returned to his retail businesses. New partners were Ed Nichols and John Ploeger. In 1982 the partners bought Lee's 51 percent share and he stayed on for a year to help in the transition.

About 1980 it was obvious that Lee and Fern would soon retire from the business. Fern had her bridge club and still arranged parties. She got her hair and nails done every week. Lee didn't play golf and you didn't want to play bridge with him. He knew how, but got no satisfaction from playing. Their son became concerned about what Lee would do in retirement. While visiting in San Diego, Lee showed interest in his son's commodore 64 computer. He took it home and got John Bohlin interested in computers. They attended a class or two. Just as in business, Lee had his old chief engineer working with him – now on the computer. When Fern was arranging a Payette High School class reunion, Lee prepared the mail-outs and easily kept the roster records. His son upgraded him to an HP computer in a year or so, and John still came to the rescue whenever he had a problem.

Lee & Fern continued traveling in winter months. Picture (456) is Lee and John Bohlin at the O. K. Coral in Tombstone, Arizona, with Wyatt Earp and "Doc" Holiday in 1981. Picture (457) is a1981 photo of Lee on the main street of Avalon, Catalina Island, California. Picture (458) Shows Fern and Lee in 1981, with Emet, Jacqueline and Frank & Vida Bork in their winter rental at Condominium at Coronado Shores in Coronado, California.

*Lee and John Bohlin visited the O. K. Corral in Tombstone,*
*Arizona, scene of the famous gun fight.*

*The Bolts visited Catalina Island, with Lee taking
in the main street scene in Avalon.*

*Fern & Lee held dinner parties at their winter
lodging apartment in Coronado Shores.*

While managing the business, and serving the city, Lee and Fern helped one family own a home they were about to lose. They helped others get jobs when most needed. In the forties, they provided Lee's parents their first refrigerator, freezer and a spray machine for their apple orchard. They helped Fern's parents buy and operate a small fruit orchard on the Emmett South slope.

The Emmett Messenger-Index published the following editorial July 15, 1983: Former Mayor, Lee Bolt, Young at 84 & Staying young. Lee Bolt, who was 84 Friday, recently returned from a salmon fishing trip in Oregon. He landed a 28-pound salmon unassisted, and added some steelhead to his catch during the trip. Friends sang greetings to the former mayor, joining him Friday for a noon luncheon at the Timbers. Mrs. Bolt cut the special day cake. The Bolts displayed a birthday card from their son and daughter-in-law, Emet and Jacqueline, of San Diego. It contained checks written in 1912 on the Emmett Bank and an old token (hinky) from the Cherry Blossom, part of a cache Jacqueline found at a flea market in San Diego.

Perhaps a major reason Lee and Fern stayed young past the life expectancy of the time, was their travels and Lee's continued fishing for those big ones. Picture (460) shows Lee with a big catch and his nephew, Don Denman, and his wife, Kristy, in 1983. In earlier years, Don's father, Kenneth Denman, and Lee were fishing buddies and close friends. Don & Kristy continued to see that Lee got his share of fishing near Medford, Oregon, and held Lee's 95th birthday party at their home. Pictures (461) and (462) show Lee and Fern with Emet, Don Denman, Lee's sister (Margaret) and the cake. The men did some catch & release fishing in the Rogue River. They all caught fish, but Lee was the only one to get a steelhead. See Picture (463). Fishing keeps people young at heart!

*On his 95th Birthday Lee shows off his catch, with Don & Kristy Denman.*

*Don & Kristy Denman hosted Lee's 95th Birthday Party at their Cady Lane home in Medford, with his sister, Margaret.*

*That 95th Birthday cake was a work of art, Fisherman and all.*

*On his birthday, Lee was the only fisherman to catch a steelhead.*

Bedrooms were either upstairs or in the basement at the Evergreen Drive home. In 1984 Lee and Fern sold that home and moved to a single-story home on East Main Street. They continued traveling a lot, and remained active in community and Church affairs.

Lee was working on trying to use sagebrush trees for the landscape in the front yard of their Main Street house. Picture (459) shows him working on those shrubs. He did get them to grow and stay healthy.

*Lee tried to get lots of unusual plants to grow.*

A big party was held for Fern's 80th birthday, April 6, 1986. Picture (464) shows her blowing out the candles, as Emet, grandson (Jon) and great grandson (Ryan) observe.

*Fern blew out the candles for her 80th birthday..*

There was a big 1994 party to celebrate Lee & Fern's 70th wedding anniversary. Picture (465) shows the huge cake enjoyed by all.

*Wow, what a cake for 70th Anniversary!*

In 1994 Lee began having health problems. Though having just renewed has driver's license (at 95) he stopped driving. Over 75 years he'd driven millions of miles, never having been involved a serious accident. He used to have a notice clearly posted in the car, reading; "This automobile is driven from the left front seat only. Those not liking the manner in which it is operated kindly note the sprig of mistletoe attached to the driver's coat tail." Fern was now in the driver's seat, and she also was an accident-free driver.

Lee had been using a medicating breathing machine once or twice a day to help his lung capacity. Now he had to have oxygen most of the time. Their son came several times, and helped choose girls to stay with them during the day. Kay Salinas and Debra Scott were wonderful. They took turns coming about 7:00 AM and leaving after evening meal. Connie Downs (from Home Health) came a couple of times a week to check on Lee and help him take a bath. With the help of these girls, Lee and Fern could continue living at home.

Lee was hospitalized a couple of times with pneumonia and had to implement exercise programs to build up his strength. Their son took over their annual bookkeeping in 1995. Satisfying two experienced bookkeepers took some adjusting. A spreadsheet program made it simple and acceptable. They had always had a Boise CPA, Mr. Brady, do their taxes. It was an old business relationship. Their son came in February or March and prepared the income tax data for Lee & Fern's review, then presenting everything to Mr. Brady.

Grandpa, Emet, ensured the children learned to ski. Picture (466). shows Jordann, Ryan and Taylor in winter 1997.

*The grandchildren learned to ski at Boise's Bogus Basin.*

By 1998 the city of Emmett had still not forgotten Lee & Fern's service to the community. Picture (467) shows the special old automobile they rode in at the traditional Cherry Festival parade. The city named a street for them, "FERNLEE" street.

*Lee & Fern were honored at the annual Cherry
festival parade, riding in an antique car.*

A big party was held for Lee's 100th birthday. Since he was born in July, a field of 40 flags was displayed in the front yard. There were about 80 people helping celebrate. Picture (468) shows Lee & Fern with their son, three grandsons and two great-grandsons.

*Lee's 1999 100th Birthday was an unusual event.*

In February 2000 Fern called their son to ask if he would come to help with the taxes. He arrived in March and organized the data. He told Fern he'd prepared everything, but could not find evidence she paid the estimated tax for September and January. She was silent for a moment, and then said "I didn't pay them". When she was told it was all left in a schedule to make it easy, she said "I know that. I didn't send them". She was silent for a minute or so, and added "I don't think people 94 and 100 years old should have to worry about this kind of stuff". Another period of silence, and she said "Besides, I don't think they deserve it". Lee had not heard this conversation, but when it was related to him, he laughed and said "No! If they don't deserve it, don't send it to 'em".

March 2000 was not a good month for the Bolts. Lee was rushed to the Emmett hospital. Their son, Jaqueline, and their grandson, Clay, came from San Diego, Jon & Cherie and the 3 grandchildren, Ryan, Jordann & Taylor, were in nearby Boise, and Lee jr. & Nell came from North Carolina. The Hospital and Doctors were wonderfully supportive, but there was little they could do for his weakness and pneumonia he'd had for 2 weeks and the COPD for years. He died at nearly 101 years of age, March 18th 2000. Three days later, the town turned out in huge numbers for his funeral. The Emmett Christian Church managed the services, including Masonic funeral rite. He was buried in the Emmett, Cemetery. Lee's funeral day was marked with U. S. flags in the front yard, as shown in Picture (469).

*Lee & Fern's Main street home was decorated with flags for his funeral day.*

The evening of the funeral, the Jon Bolt family, Clay and Jacqueline returned to Boise. Lee jr. & Nell were on their way back to North Carolina. Fern, her son and niece, Mary Jane Buck, sat down for a dinner prepared by Kay Salinas. Fern was having severe stomach pains. Lying down didn't help, so it was off to the Hospital. The prognosis was not good. She had heart problems and severe intestinal blockage. She died April 1, 2000 with the family present. After the Christian Church funeral, she was buried beside Lee in their plot at Emmett Cemetery.

Picture (470) Shows the plaque installed at Mount Soledad Veteran's Memorial near San Diego, California. It honors the military service of 5 Bolt men, Pvt Leland Eddy Bolt U. S. Army (World War I), his grandfather 1st Lt Charles Bolt State of Iowa Militia during the Civil War, son CAPT Leland Emet Bolt U. S. Navy (Korea & Viet Nam), his grandson Sp-4 Leland Emet Bolt jr. U. S. Army (Cold War), and his great-grandson Sgt Ryan Mabe Bolt U. S. Marine Corps (Iraq & Afghanistan).

*Bolt military service plaque on Mount Soledad Veteran's Memorial in San Diego, California.*

The drop-out (in his last year of college) and the girl he married after her high school graduation were abundantly successful, and contributed so much to their family, the business and their community.

# SECTION 2

# The Business

Lee's accounting training and experience at Standard Oil Company prepared him well for the financial end of business operations. He said "You have to know if you are making money. That may seem silly, but you would be surprised how many do not know". This experience was further enhanced paying farmers for their crops in Washington and Idaho 1924 - 1928. Returning to Payette, Idaho, in 1928, he got further business experience at the F. H. Hogue Inc. main office. In 1932 he became the Bookkeeper at the F. H. Hogue office in Emmett, Idaho. The Hogue business and other local growers grew Apples, Pears, Italian Prunes, Peaches, Apricots and Cherries. Hogue had 3 farms of about 40 acres each. During the harvest season they prepared and sent their own and other growers' fruit to market. The sales were directed and negotiated by Fern's uncle, Scott Brubaker, out of the main office in Payette.

Lee observed how the fruit was packed by women, one box or basket at a time. The fruit was dumped on each woman's table. Their finished packages were labeled with the F. H. Hogue Falcon brand, and transported to refrigerated railroad cars for shipment to markets throughout the country.

Apple processes were the most complex, because they had to be sprayed many times while growing, to prevent worms and tree destroying insects. The apple spray was arsenate of lead. So the processing for marketing included washing in solutions of muriatic acid, followed by thoroughly washing away of the residue. Women arranged apples around a circular plate and a paper collar (with temporary metal support) was inserted over the apple packed cylinder. After filling with apples, the metal packing cylinder was removed and a bushel basket pushed over the filled paper collar. The basket was then inverted, exposing the carefully packed circular rings of apples. The basket lid was installed and the bushel of apples labeled, ready for marketing. This process was in need of improved efficiency and quality.

By 1938 Lee knew all the growers in the area, and demonstrated his ability to manage the growing, harvesting, packing and shipment operations. He was promoted to Manager of Emmett operations. The first order of business was to create an "assembly line" for processing and shipping fruit to market. One of his great "stokes of luck" was that John Bohlin came by, asking for a job. Picture (475) is Lee showing the high quality package of fresh cherries, with the F. H. Hogue Inc. Falcon brand.

*Lee with a beautiful crate of Falcon brand cherries.*

Under Lee's direction, Hogue's 120 acres of orchards in Emmett grew to 200 acres. He helped other growers to retire aging orchards and plant varieties to best meet future market demands. This was a key to valley fruit grower success. New trees take 2 or 3 years to produce enough fruit yield to be profitable. Also, the market demands change. For example, in the 1930s and 1940s Winesap and Johnathan apples were popular. Today, you don't see them. Varieties of delicious apples are still popular, but Gala, Fuji and other varieties are in demand. Lee worked with the Salesman, Scott Brubaker, to predict the variety changes. He managed future Hogue orchard upgrades and advised other growers to meet market demands. Picture (476) is Lee at his typewriter in the office. Hat and overcoat were needed, as there was no heat in winter. One of Lee's rules was to not do business the same way every year. There had to be things that needed improving, like bins and lift trucks replacing boxes and hand trucks. Such additions improved processes and saved time and expenses.

*The manager in winter, was his own secretary.*

The beginning process for maraschino cherries was added to F. H. Hogue Emmett products about 1940. Royal Ann cherries were yellow and dull reddish color, and not popular in the fresh cherry market, but they were good for the maraschino market. The Hogue process put the fruit, as picked in the orchards, into wood barrels in a sulfurous acid solution that bleached the fruit. In this condition, they were sold to firms like Del Monte and Libby for completing the maraschino process of washing, pitting and adding artificial red coloring. During World War II, potatoes were grown on leased land to help feed the domestic and military demands. Frozen pie cherries were added to the product line. This operation packed in 5 gallon cans the Mount Morenci variety of cherries all washed, pitted and stems removed. Sugar was added and they were frozen. Upon thawing cherries were ready to pour into the pie shell and bake.

Picture shows Lee & Fern presenting a production box of Cherries to Senator Welker during Emmett's 1956 Cherry Festival.

*Honored guests received boxes of cherries during the annual Emmett festival.*

In 1962 Mr. Hogue had died and his heirs decided to manage the Emmett fruit business. Lee was terminated at F. H. Hogue, Inc., but didn't miss any time in the Fruit business. He found partners, John Bohlin and Ernie Radke, and started Emmett Valley Fruits, Inc. The partners were chosen for their key positions needed at the new company. John Bohlin was the indispensable Chief Engineer that got the fruit processing equipment "up and running" in time for the next harvest. Ernie was the experienced salesman. Picture (478) shows Lee in his new Emmett Valley Fruits office, starting the new company. Fern was the office manager, assisted by her sister, Iris, in the harvest season. Fern's niece, Mary Jane (Collier) Buck, became the packing crew superintendent. In a couple of years the company was doing $3 million in gross sales and growing.

*Lee in his new Office .*

The new building at 220 East Park is shown in Picture (445). It included packing and refrigerated storage facilities. Pictures (446 and 447) are the utility truck and one of the fruit bin trucks for the new business. Picture (448) is the new fertilizer business, for supporting grower needs.

*The new packing & storage facility.*

*The new business supervisor truck.*

*Trucks haul fruit bins from orchard to packing facility.*

*The business included a fertilizer service to growers.*

Emmett Valley Fruits was appointed sales and service agent for Hardie spray machines, and added service and repair of such equipment. Their new plant was able to process 600 barrels of brined cherries for sale to maraschino cherry processors.

Picture (477) shows Lee supervising the first apples packed by the new Emmett Valley Fruits. Having peaked in available Emmett fruit products, the company convinced the Symms' Sunny Slope Farms to have their fruit packed and sold by Emmett Valley Fruits. The facilities had to expand. The new Emmett Valley Fruits, built in 1967, was a larger modern production and storage facility. See Picture (452).

*Emmett Valley Fruits had efficient packing operations.*

*New warehouse and packing facilities were built in 1967.*

About 1979 John Bohlin and Ernie Radke chose to sell their partnership shares. John stayed on as Chief Engineer, and Ernie returned to his retail businesses. New partners were Ed Nichols and John Ploeger. In 1982 the partners bought Lee's 51 percent share, and he stayed on for a year to help in the transition.

Lee was the motivating force for the increasing F. H. Hogue fruit production in the Emmett Valley. Having been given notice near the end of 1961 that he was being replaced, he quickly reacted by getting the partners, financing, facilities and equipment for a new fruit production and servicing operation. It was all done in record time, ready for the 1962 fruit harvest. He directed the expansion to acquire new growers every year, and became the largest fruit packing, sales and service company in the valley.

# SECTION 3

# Serving the City

Lee Bolt had built the Emmett Operations of the F. H. Hogue Fruit Company into one of the most profitable businesses in the area. One day in 1945 a couple of citizens asked him to run for City Council. After discussions about his not being (or desiring to be) a politician, he agreed and was elected to the Emmett City Council. Picture (474) shows Lee with Mayor D. O. Thurman and fellow Councilmen Frank Bork, Merle Green, Walt Stanzack, Lloyd Redfelt and Basil Harrison. He observed how the Council seemed to avoid the controversial, and found the city was in serious financial condition. As an experienced accountant, he became keenly aware of the city's backlog of infrastructure maintenance and other unusual needs.

*Lee joined the Emmett City Council*

In 1953 he was urged to run for Mayor, and was elected. The first order of business was to ensure understanding of the city income and expenses. He contracted with Charlie Brady, a Boise CPA, to attend Council meetings and audit tax distributions and expenditures of each city department. It was found that, due to an administrative error, the city was not receiving the correct share of tax revenues. Finding deficient expenditures, the Mayor and Council established departmental budgets, and ensured all departments lived within them. The City attorney, Lou Gorrono, ensured compliance and advised on legal matters. Lee said the city is "big Business" and needs capable people in City Hall, with knowledge of accounting. He said it was taxpayer money that ran the city, and we must ensure wise expenditure of those funds.

Second, the Mayor and Council established a working arrangement to ensure that their actions had broad support of the citizens. Any citizen could address the Council, so extra meetings were often necessary. In some cases, Councilmen and/or volunteers got direct public "feedback" and helped shape actions with broad public support. The needs were huge, like:

1. The system of Individual responsibility for garbage disposal was not working. Compulsory garbage collection had to be implemented and funded. Many were opposed, saying they did their disposal job properly and did not want to pay for having the city do it. After hearing all citizens at Council meetings, the Mayor engaged volunteers to talk individually with everyone. Though some still disagreed, the overwhelming majority accepted the new fee and collection rules.

2. City raw sewage was dumped into the Payette River, in violation of Federal law. Citizens agreed that a sewage treatment plant was needed, but didn't want it near their property! Council worked with citizens to acquire a site and implement an acceptable plan. Property west of the Boise Cascade Mill was purchased and the lagoons dug. A new main sewer line from downtown Emmett to the new facility was included. This was a costly and time consuming project.

3. About 75% of the city streets were unpaved dirt or gravel, with dust in summer and rutted quagmires in winter. The city had huge manpower and assets devoted to street maintenance. Paving

would be hugely expensive. Council and Citizens combined to find an acceptable solution at lower cost. Each time the city graded and made a road acceptable, a surface of sand and fine gravel was added. Then a coating of Asphalt oil was applied. In about 3 years all roads were as good as paved, without major debt obligations. The city saved on annual maintenance as well.

4.  The state wanted to make the Washington Street (highway 16) through town wider and replace the aged 1927 bridge over the Payette River. This involved a couple hundred property owners, many of whom didn't want to lose a few feet of property. After hearing all citizens at Council meetings, the Mayor, Council and volunteers talked individually with everyone affected. Though some still disagreed, the overwhelming majority accepted the new state highway plan.

5.  The City facilities (Clerk, Chief of Police, jail, meeting room and fire engine) had outgrown the tiny downtown office building. The Mayor and Council worked out a $1 per year lease with the County for use of the vacant former Mary Secor County Hospital building.

6.  Emmett had also outgrown the small public library in a downtown office building, and desperately needed a new public library. The city could not afford both a new city hall and library. The Deal with the County Commissioners (to rent the old Hospital Building for $1 per year) meant the new library could be built at 2nd and Hayes Streets. Councilman Olberding made a Deal with the Catholic Church to furnish the lot for the Library, if the city paved the parking lot for combined Library and Church use.

7.  The Mayor and Council took the time to get acquainted with Sister Cities. Mayors and dignitaries of surrounding cities came for the annual Cherry Festival and the Gem County Rodeo. Dinners were at the Bolt home, and Fern loved to be the hostess. Dignitaries rode in the Parades. This continued 18 years. The city found friends that at times proved most helpful. For example, the engineer on the payroll of another city performed the required engineering assessment of Emmett's new sewage disposal plant plans. Picture (484) shows Boise First Lady, Mrs. Jay Amyx,

welcoming Emmett's Mayor and First Lady to a 1968 conference of Mayors from surrounding cities.

8. The park facilities on Main Street at Johns Avenue were repaired and improved. The old band shell stage was refurbished. The Swimming Pool was built in the park for Emmett and County residents. Boise Cascade and many others assisted. Wells were drilled in the City Park and Cemetery. Sprinkler equipment was purchased and installed in both. Park Restrooms and Tennis Courts were upgraded.

MRS. JAY AMYX, left, wife of the mayor of Boise, welcomed

*Boise First Lady, Mrs. Amyx, greets Mayor & Mrs. Bolt.*

These and other infrastructure improvements were made possible by the accountability established in the funding and budget control process and the tireless work of the Mayor, Council and volunteers. Citizens regularly addressed the Council with valid concerns and ideas. One of Lee's teen-age nephews went to a Council meeting or two. He remarked about the way he drew out problem definitions, patiently listened to all citizens, identified alternatives, and guided the decisions to constructive solutions that nearly all could accept.

The Mayor and First Lady had a Jeep ride in the 1956 Cherry Festival parade, as shown in Picture (482). Picture (483) shows Lee & Fern presenting the traditional box of cherries to Idaho's Senator Welker, the parade Grand Marshall.

*Mayor and Mrs. Bolt rode a Jeep in the Cherry Festival parade.*

*Senator Welker is presented a box of Emmett cherries.*

A good summary of Lee's executive ability and leadership appeared in the Emmett Messenger-Index 7 March 1957, as follows: *Emmett has been outstandingly blessed through the years with excellent city administrations. Administrations have varied in impact, leadership, and accomplishment, but each succeeding one has produced competent, honorable men well qualified by sense of responsibility and willingness to give unselfishly of their time and talent in service.*

*The present city council can perhaps in terms of service be termed outstanding among outstanding councils. Our comment here takes note of Emmett's mayor, L. E. Bolt, prompted at this particular time by an example which appeared last Monday of his ability to get things done. Soon after annexation of five new additions to the city, a suggestion was made that a special official census of the city on the basis of its greater area might find a larger population base for the allocation of state liquor, highway and other revenues due the city. A significant attribute of Mayor Bolt is that he does not let things dangle. He doesn't make hasty decisions, but he doesn't fail or neglect to make them. He makes up his mind and acts. In the same way, he takes care of details that another may might let slide.*

*And so at last Monday's council meeting there was read a reply from the census bureau, detailing procedures and costs for a special Emmett census. All preliminary details already had been attended to, including the preparation of official maps for the census. Mayor Bolt had ascertained the consensus of the council. There was a quick, informed, easy decision, and the census apparently is in the works in less time than it would take others to wonder if it might be a good idea.*

*This executive ability, together with a ready willingness and capacity to serve unstintingly, has been extremely valuable to the city of Emmett. Following service on the council, Mayor Bolt is completing his second term as Emmett's chief executive. He has not yet made known whether or not he will be a candidate for re-election next month. As strong Emmett partisans, we suggest that another term under Mayor Bolt would be a very good thing for Emmett, and we express the hope that he will consent to run again.*

Lee did not run for another term. In 1959 he was succeeded by Mr. George Yost, his friend and main competitor in the fruit business. In 1964 Lee was elected Mayor again, and served until 1974.

The informal association of local area Mayors was a positive step in achieving efficiencies in Government. The Mayors held a race at the opening of

Firebird Raceway along state highway 16, on the road to Star and Boise. Lee represented Emmett, and found the big city folks seemed to have better cars than what he had been provided. So, he turned to "skill and cunning". By "getting the jump" on the others and maneuvering aggressively he defeated all but Caldwell Mayor Coley. It was close! Even though Lee came in second, he got the great big trophy shown in Picture (485).

*Second place won a big trophy.*

Picture (486) shows Fern, as Emmett's First Lady, presenting an apple to Louise Shadduck, Director of Idaho State Commerce & Development. The real gift was a bushel basket of apples provided later.

*Fern presented the apple to Idaho Director of Commerce & Development.*

Picture (487) is the Emmett Messenger-Index 10 January 1974 picture of retiring Mayor L. E. Bolt, left center passing the office to incoming Mayor Rod Morgan. City councilmen crowded in to get a closer look at the miniature gavel bequeathed to the new mayor. Bolt also presented a shiny "Emmett Mayor" badge, similar to a police badge, which he said had been found in the old city hall building and is a memento of earlier days when mayors actually were principal law enforcement officers. Councilmen, from left are, Dr. William B. Jewell, Royce Fuhriman, Clarence Mitchell, Duane Hodgins, Dr. Larry Downer, and Jim Stroud. Picture (480) is a picture of the retiring Mayor and First Lady upon retirement from city service in 1974.

*The new City Council honors the outgoing Mayor in 1974.*

*The Bolt were honored for nearly 20 years of service to the city.*

Council unanimously adopted a resolution recognizing retiring Mayor L. E. Bolt for astute, dignified and dedicated service, epitomizing the highest quality of leadership. Mayor Rod Morgan proclaimed Thursday, January 17, as Lee Bolt Day in Emmett, with a public recognition banquet scheduled that evening under auspices of the Gem County Chamber of Commerce.

What was it these citizens saw in Lee, and why did he keep serving? He received $5 per meeting as Council Member, and $25 per month as Mayor, and resisted change in compensation. He did it for the challenges - what he could do for the city. And challenges there were! Many problems were satisfied with broad citizen support. Lee and his wife, Fern, entertained visiting mayors and dignitaries (e.g. Paul Harvey, Harmon Killebrew, etc,) at the annual Cherry Festival and Gem County Rodeo. These entertainment obligations were a delight for Fern, who loved to host entertainment. She had large sets of dishes, silverware, tables and tablecloths. No paper and plastic! The menus were always good and she arranged help, either volunteer or paid. But, there was no city budget for entertaining.

Perhaps there is no more fitting tribute to Lee's community service than the editorial in the Emmett Messenger-Index edition of January 24, 1974: "When Bolt retired from City Office this month, he left Emmett a double heritage, he left the City in sound financial condition, well current on its facility needs, and with a remarkably low taxing level; and he left qualified and experienced people to carry on in behalf of the City in his stead. I think it only fair to mention that without the help of our City Attorney, Lou Gorrono, and our Accountant, Charlie Brady, all these things would not have been accomplished. They gave the City much more than they were paid to themselves."

The Emmett Messenger–Index Newspaper is quoted to show the thoughts at the time, and to show how the local newspaper supported Lee and his City Council, Attorney and Accountant. The editor of this newspaper was a strong member of the opposite political party. This was about good governance, not politics.

# SECTION 4

# References

1. I REMEMBER, DO YOU?, An Ideals Publication, 3rd Printing, Milwaukee, WI, 1973
2. Emmett Messenger Newspaper:

   a. One of the Most Interesting People I Have Met, by Sam Riggs, 5 May 1955
   b. News &Views, Two Good Terms Deserve, 7 March 1957
   c. Trio Launches New Packing Firm in Emmett, 25 January 1962
   d. In Plain Sight, 30 April 1964
   e. Bolt Family Holiday Reunion picture and description 28 December 1967
   f. News & Views, 24 January 1974, To Lee & Fern with affection,
   g. Former Mayor, Lee Bolt, Stays Young at 84, 15 July 1983
   h. Obituaries, Leland & Fern Bolt 2000

3. State of Idaho, County of Payette, Marriage License, Leland Eddy Bolt and Fern Leoline Brubaker, 22 May 1924.
4. State of Idaho Birth Certificate, Leland Emet Bolt
5. State of Idaho Certificate of Marriage, Leland Eddy Bolt & Fern Leoline Brubaker
6. State of Idaho, Death Certificate, Leland Eddy Bolt
7. State of Idaho, Death Certificate, Fern Leoline (Brubaker) Bolt
8. State of Idaho Marriage Certificate, Leland Emet Bolt & Jacqueline Joyce Barker
9. State of Idaho, Governor's Certificate of L. E. Bolt in Th District Magistrates Commission 7 January 1970.
10. U. S. Army Discharge, Pvt Leland Eddy Bolt

11. Armed Forces DD-214 CAPT Leland E. Bolt USN
12. Armed Forces DD-214 Sp4 Leland Emet Bolt jr. U. S Army
13. Armed Forces DD-214 Sgt Ryan Mabe Bolt, USMC
14. State of Iowa, Charles Bolt Appointment as 1st Lt, Iowa Militia.
15. Idaho Statesman Newspaper, Obituary, Leland Eddy Bolt
16. Idaho Statesman Newspaper, Obituary, Fern Leoline (Brubaker) Bolt
17. Idaho Statesman Newspaper, Man of the Year 1972,
18. Letter, Lee & Fern Bolt, 10 September 1993, re: Accomplishments during my nearly 20 years as Mayor of Emmett
19. Lee's 90th Birthday Book & Picture Album, 1989
20. Fern's 90th Birthday Book & Picture Album, 1996
21. Lee's 95th Birthday Book & Picture Album, 1994
22. Two Black Canyon Articles from 9 May 1924 issue of Newspapers, Courtesy of "Rick" Hogue, from his mother's historical collection.
23. Letter (email) from Emmett City Clerk, re: Leland Eddy Bolt years of service on the City Council and as Mayor, dated 4 November 2014.
24. Biography, Leland Eddy Bolt by his son, Leland Emet Bolt
25. Notes on the life of Fern (Brubaker) Bolt, by her
26. Draft Registration (D.S.S. Form 2), Leland Eddy Bolt 16 February 1942
27. Notice of Classification (D.S.S. Form57) Leland Eddy Bolt 1 August 1944.

# APPENDIX A

# Genealogical Roots of Leland Eddy Bolt and Fern Leoline Brubaker

In writing the story of Leland and Fern, it is believed that the ancestral history has much bearing on their lives and accomplishments. This Appendix shows the genealogical line to their grandparents. The proof of those roots has not been even among their ancestors. For example, the Eddy line has been proven back to William Eddye, the 1591 to 1616 Vicar of St. Dunstan's Church in Cranbrook, Kent, England. But the Fulton line has only been proven to John Fulton and Sally M. (Green) Fulton, parents of Fern's grandfather, George Reynolds Fulton. Reliably traced ancestors are presented for each of the 8 families of the grandparents.

**A-1 The Bolts.** Many researchers have documented our Bolt line, dating back to John Bolt (born in Virginia in 1750). Until 2005 little could be found to substantiate the parents of our John. The descendants of Robert Bolt (born 1910 in Ireland) found that Robert had a son (believed to be named John) born about 1750. That was the year of our John Bolt's birth, according to his gravestone. DNA testing of males from both Bolt lines gave an extremely strong indication of a common ancestor. On that basis we accepted John as the missing child of Robert's family. 15 November 1736, in London, Robert Bolt stole from Thomas Stanthrop at the Crown Inn, a hat worth 2 Shillings & 6 Pence. He was sentenced to transportation and sailed December 1736 to the British colony of Virginia on the ship Dorsetshire. The ship arrived in the Rappahannock with 139 convicts. Robert was an indentured servant from 1737 to 1743. Robert and his wife, Rachel, married about 1741 in Virginia. Their children:

- Mary, born 12 April 1744
- **John, born 6 June 1750**
- Sarah, born 3 May 1753
- James, born 3 April 1755
- Franklin, born 31 August 1757
- Unknown male, Born 9 February 1760

## Second Generation

Our John Bolt (1750 - 1832) was born in Virginia. He married his first wife, Elizabeth Yeargin about 1771 in Virginia. She was born about 1754 and died about 1802. Their Children;

- Winifred, born in Patrick County Virginia about 1771 and died in 1825 at Walnut Creek, Ohio. She married William Garrett 8 October 1792 in Cabell County, Virginia.
- **Charles Bolt** was born about 1772 in Grayson County, Virginia. See Third Generation below for children and our line of Bolts.
- James, born about 1775 in Virginia and died about 1851. He married Hannah Bloss. James moved from Virginia to Huntington, West Virginia, and then on to Kentucky where he had a 100 acre farm near where his Brother, Isaac, established Bolt's Fork. He later moved the family to Indiana. (Letter from Susan Campbell, dated 30 Jan 2001)
- John jr., was born about 1778 in Virginia and died about 1862. He is buried in the Carpenter Cemetery. He married Rebecca Dillard 8 January 1807 in Patrick County, Virginia. Like his brother, Charles, John jr. was a trader in lands, who managed well all his life - at least until in old age he gave his property away. Folklore on Burk's Fork is that John jr. was known as "Mean Johnny", and not without cause. He was said to have waylaid William McPeak and killed him. There was no prosecution and little, if any, evidence. But, 150 years later the tale was still repeated. In 1839 John jr. and Rebecca separated. John placed much of his personal property in trust for the use of Rebecca

and the younger children, who were then staying with her. The 1840 census enumerated Rebecca and the younger children with Isaac Bolt's family. About this time, John gave most of his land to his children, and was left landless. He is recorded at the age of 82 in the 1860 Carroll County census, living with his son, Thomas. It is believed that he died a few years later, and is buried in an unmarked grave at Fremont.

- Elizabeth, born about 1786 in Virginia and date of death is unknown. She married Burnett Harris in 1806 in Patrick County, Virginia.
- Isaac, born 13 October 1789 in Montgomery County, Virginia and died 13 July 1860 at Boltsfork, Lawrence County, Kentucky. He is buried in the Bolt Cemetery at Boltsfork. He married Elizabeth Booten. Isaac and Elizabeth were prominent in the history of Kentucky, where they lived nearly all their lives. Isaac was one of the "founding fathers" of Lawrence County, Kentucky, and did early surveys. He was instrumental in establishing Bolt's Fork (later became Boltsfork). Isaac was an early Lawrence County Commissioner and Justice of the Peace. He was Sheriff of the County for a period about 1839. The Governor appointed him to "lay out" the county into districts, and enlisted his help to stop the practice of dueling. (Letter from Maxine Bolt to Leland Bolt, dated 8 Nov 1999) Isaac served as an Army Lieutenant in the War of 1812, in Moses Conkleton's Company, 4th Regiment, Virginia Militia. He ultimately achieved the rank of Major. (Boyd County News History article, 6 Feb 1975, Ref. 128) and State of Kentucky Widow's Pension Claim, dated 5 April 1871 (part of Ref 159)

John's wife, Elizabeth, died before 1803. John married second Celia Amos in Patrick County, Virginia, in 1803. Her birth date is unknown. Their children were:

- Elias, born in 1805 and died in 1886.
- Lewis (twin of Elias), born in 1805 and death date unknown.
- Martha, born in1809 and death date unknown.

# Third Generation

Charles Bolt, son of John Bolt was born about 1772 in Grayson County, Virginia. In 1796 he married Mary Ann Barnard (or Bernard) (b. 1778 and d. 1830). He was an ambitious man, dealing in many hundreds of acres of land from 1800 to 1828 in Patrick, Grayson and Floyd Counties, Virginia, and Stokes County North Carolina. He acquired two or 3 slaves in 1800. Charles helped the older children get their starts in life, but lost his wife, Mary, sometime before 1830. Financial problems came upon Charles in the 1830s. In 1833 he sold the last of his Floyd County property, and lost the Grayson County property to foreclosure in 1835. The last record of Charles in Virginia was a June 1835 bill of sale to pay his son, Hiram, for a crop of corn. He had become convinced that slavery was wrong and freed his. Speculation is that he went to Missouri. Children of Charles and Mary Bolt:

- Charles Jr., born 1796 and died in1876
- Hiram, born 16 March 1799 an died 9 March 1859
- **John, born 9 April 1802 and died 30 January 1876**
- James, born 22 November 1805 and died 14 June 1848
- Lucy B., born about 1806 and date died unknown

John Bolt, born 9 April 1802, met and married Karenhappuch Horton 12 October 1820 in Stokes County, North Carolina. He was trained as a wheelwright, under an apprenticeship with her father, Jacob Horton. 18 January 1822, Jacob Horton became a grandfather for the first time with the birth of Pollie Bolt (born to John and Karenhappuch Bolt). In the spring of 1832 John, Karenhappuch and their baby, Pollie, joined the Jacob Horton family in their move to Highland County, Ohio, where many of his relatives and many of their Society of Friends had located. It is said that on an Ohio River steamboat, Jacob Horton saw himself in a full length mirror for the first time. He extended his hand, saying: "Thy face is familiar but I cannot quite recall thy name". The first steamboat had come to the Ohio River in 1811, but the better ones came with the "Washington" in 1816. In Highland County, Ohio, John applied his wheelwright skills in the specialized art of creating spinning wheels. He made all the furniture for their new home, and expanded his trade to include cabinet work. He also taught school in Hillsboro, Ohio, and was an avid student of the Bible. In 1840 John and Karenhappuch moved to Indiana, settling in Noblesville, Hamilton County.

In 1855 John and family moved on to Montgomery County, Iowa. He bought land in Sections 29, 30 & 31 of Pilot Grove Township. The 1856 census shows the family living in West Township and having been in the state less than a year.

17 November 1856, at the term of the District Court, John Bolt was a member of the first Grand Jury. Their first action was on a proposed indictment of Isaac Bolt and J. T. Patterson for fighting. The vote apparently was against indictment, but the fighters "got a good scare" and behaved themselves afterward. In September 1859 Montgomery County held its first Fair at Frankfort in the old school house and surrounding fields. John Bolt showed cattle and premium mares. He raised fine horses, and grew premium apples as well.

In 1861 John Bolt was Trustee of Frankfort Township. In 1862 his son Charles Bolt was elected County Sheriff, and James Riley Horton was re-elected County Judge. In 1865 the county seat was moved to Red Oak.

Jacob Horton's daughter, Karenhappuch, and her husband, John Bolt, followed her parental Quaker teachings. Though John Bolt was never a Quaker or a member of any church, he was a great student of the Bible. He was Frankfort Township Trustee during 1861, until the elections were held in October. Major duties of the Trustee were paying bounty on wolf and wildcat scalps, which had gone down from $1.50 to $1.00 each. John stayed close to his farming, producing crops, apples and animals. He was elected to the Montgomery County Board of Supervisors in 1868, representing Frankfort Township, and served 1869 thru 1870. A Grant Township petition for addition of more sections lost by one vote of the Supervisors 6 January 1869. John Bolt voted against. The Railroad commenced a To Defend suit against the County, which passed by a 7 to 1 vote. The lone no voter was John Bolt. In January 1870 the County Clerk statement of payments shows John Bolt was allowed for Board Attendance: $10 for 4 days, plus $1.20 for 10 miles travel.

Though no pictures of John Bolt were found, Picture (A1) shows Karenhappuch about 1860.

*Picture (H1) Karenhappuch Horton, the Quaker lady.*

When John died in January 1876, he was buried beside his wife, Karenhappuch, in the Frankfort Cemetery. The gravestones were identical in size and shape, with a weeping willow tree engraved above each name. The town of Frankfort has disappeared without a trace. The cemetery is all that's left.

Children of John & Karenhappuch Bolt are:

- Pollie, born 19 January 1822 in Stokes County, North Carolina. She married a man with surname Binegar.
- Letha Ruth (1823 – 1883)
- Malinda (1827 -1849)
- Phebe Jane (b. 1829)
- **Charles, born (1831 – 1912) See Chapter 1, section 1.**
- Sallie Ann (1834 – 1835)
- Jacob Dentatus (b. 1837)
- William Lee B. 1839 & died in infancy.
- Ira Webster (1841 - 1893)
- Kara Ann, born (b. 1842)

References:

1.  Alderman, John Perry; Carroll 1765-1815 The Settlements, Alderman Books, Hillsville, VA, 1985
2.  Martin, Nina Leona, & Bolt, Ronald Ben, Bolt Americana; self-published; Copyright 1968.
3.  Cemetery Records of Carroll County, VA, (Rev. 2001), Susan Burrow Editor, Greenway Press Inc. Baltimore, MD
4.  Virginia Marriage Index, 1740 – 1850, 16 April 1999 on line search for surname BOLT, by Leland E. Bolt, San Diego, CA
5.  Watson, Mattie, Genealogy Sheets; Elwood, Hiram and Ira Webster Bolt family Data 1986
6.  Watson, Mattie, Letter 1994, Additional relatives & pictures
7.  Headstones, Frankfort Cemetery, Iowa, by Mattie Watson 12 February 1987, John Bolt & his wife, Karenhappuch (Horton) Bolt.
8.  History of Montgomery County, Iowa 1881, published by Iowa Historical and Biographical Co., Des Moines, IA.
9.  Bolt WPA Cemetery Records 1938 – 1941, Volume 1
10. Letter from Maxine Bolt to Leland Bolt dated 9 Nov 1999.
11. Chris Bolt 1999 report of markings observed on John Bolt gravestone and Carrol County, VA, Genealogical Society, death date of 18 March 1832, and age at time of death as 81 years, 11 months and 24 days.
12. 16 April 1999 search of Ancestry.Com data base for surname BOLT in the Virginia Marriage Index, 1740 – 1850
13. John & Karenhappuch Bolt Headstones in Frankfort Cemetery, near Red Oak, Iowa.
14. Boyd County, Kentucky, News History article 6 February 1975. (Ref. 128)
15. State of Kentucky Widow's Pension Claom, dated 5 April 1871 (part of Ref. 159)

**A-2 The Hewitts.** Joseph W. Hewitt (1764 – 1846), married Elizabeth Meredith (1784 – 1853) 1810 in Queen Anne County, Maryland. Picture (A2) is a picture of Joseph, probably from the early 1800s. Their Children:

- Elizabeth (1811 – 1837)
- Mary "Polly" (1813 – 1894)
- Joseph Meredith Hewitt (1817 – 1877)
- Sarah (1820 - 1848)
- Moses Hines (1823 – 1884).

Joseph W. Hewitt.

**Joseph Meredith Hewitt (1817 – 1877)** & Sarah Harris (1819 – 1910) married in1838 in Shelby County, Indiana. Their children:

- Francis Marion (1839 – 1930),
- **Margaret Ann Hewitt (1841 – 1932),**
- William Wallis (1844 – 1854),
- Benjamin Harris (1846 – died in infancy),
- Moses Hines (1849 – 1900),
- Mary Elizabeth (1849 – 1907) twin of Moses Hines,
- Sarah Marie (1853 – 1854)
- Joseph Warren (1856 – 1927)
- Henry Bodley (1858 – 1858)
- Thomas Wiley (1863 – 1942)

Pictures (A3) and (A4) are pictures of Joseph Meredith Hewitt and Sarah Harris.

Joseph Meredith Hewitt and Sarah Harris

Sarah Harris.

Thomas Wiley Hewitt married Edith Nutting. They had a daughter, Grace, and a son, Harry Hewitt. An Interesting story about Harry Hewitt by Blane Stubblefield was used in a Memorial to Harry by his sister, Grace Hewitt Evans, at Christmas 1957. Harry lived nearly 40 years in the Wallowa Mountain country of Northeast Oregon & Southeast Washington (Joseph, Enterprise, Halfway and Richland). Thousands of people knew him, because he was almost a doctor, but not quite! At Medical School he was within 6 months of his MD degree when he became a Medical Sergeant during World War I. He returned to the Richland, Washington, area and worked for money to go back to Medical School. He "mucked" the gold mines at Cornucopia and forked binder bundles in harvest fields. Then Doctor Fred Wilson put him to work in the Drug Store at Halfway. "Doc" found he could get a Pharmacist's license. The Doctor and Harry started a drugstore at Richland. Then there was no time to go back to school. When people got sick they sent for Harry Hewitt, the young man who was almost a Doctor. Harry would go see them any time of day or night. But, he could only "advise" them how to get well. After being careful to say that he could not prescribe medicine and could not do surgery, he'd say "but, maybe I can help. What seems to be the problem?" Since he wasn't a licensed MD he could not send bills. So he didn't get paid. He had none of the glory of MDs. They called him "Doc", but not Doctor Hewitt! All he had on his office wall was a pharmacist's license.

Women up in the timber and bench lands had babies at home. The scene is depicted in many novels: Aunt Mamie, the midwife, in the lamp-lighted kitchen with a wash boiler full of hot water. But in Pine Valley and Eagle Valley they had both Aunt Mamie and "Doc" Hewitt. After all, a man with only 6 months remaining to get his medical degree must know something about birth giving. Besides, you didn't get a bill from him. Just buy a few things from his drugstore. In addition, "Doc" Hewitt was good company. He was a happy man, who made people happy. If something went wrong, like you got a lot of bills and lost your job, he would insist that a happy outcome was imminent and explain why! He made life seem like a stage play, in which everything is wonderful and easy to manage. Perhaps his size was one factor. A big man can make people feel inferior or unimportant, but "Doc" Hewitt was a little guy (only 5 feet tall). His size and mild, confident manner made people proud to have an important friend, an almost Doctor, and a pharmacist who knew all the mysteries of medical chemistry. A pharmacist is a responsible man, who is not allowed even one mistake.

Harry Hewitt used spare time to roll his snare drum and bong the base in his back room. He even became a member of Lawrence Estes' Orchestra, out of Baker City, Oregon. He was piping for dances a hundred miles around. He had rhythm in his heart, and loved to feel the Grange Halls rock to his time, but he probably enjoyed getting paid. For standing vigil all night with a man who stuck his hand in the business end of a threshing machine, he collected nothing but "thanks, Doc". But, for the fun of making music until dawn blazed on the hilltops, he could take home a ten dollar gold piece and something extra (like cameras, films, tripods, lenses). He got to be one of the best known photographers in Baker County. Years later, when the all-American controversy over dams in the Hells Canyon started, he became the principal lens man of Hells Canyon, which begins 35 miles from his Richland Drug Store. While others sat on foam rubber and leaned out of car doors to shoot rough country scenes, "Doc" got up on his two and a half foot legs and went for the hard to get pictures.

Harry Hewitt's Drugstore prospered and money came his way. But, success didn't make him any trouble at all. A highlight in later years was when his sister took him back to Red Oak, Iowa. There, the Army fired a salute to the World War I Medical Sergeant, who was almost a Doctor. When he died, it was the easy way. He made no alarm or fuss, and didn't even turn on the night light.

**Margaret Ann Hewitt (1841 – 1932)** married Charles Bolt (see Chapter 1, The Grandparents, Section 1)

# References:

1. Martin, Nina Leona, & Bolt, Ronald Ben, Bolt Americana; self-published; Copyright 1968.
2. Bolt, Benjamin Darius, To My Children; unpublished working papers for his children, documentation of his 1920 – 1950 research.
3. Headstones, Hewitt Cemetery, Red Oak, Iowa, Photograph by Leland Emet Bolt 1992, Joseph Meredith. Hewitt Esq. & wife Sarah (Harris) Hewitt.
4. Obituary, Sarah (Harris) Hewitt, Red Oak Express Newspaper 25 February 1910 Page 1, Col. 2. - Done
5. Obituary, J. W. Hewitt, Esq., Red Oak Express Newspaper 8 March 1877 – Done
6. Certificate of death, J. W. Hewitt; issued by County Registrar, Montgomery County, Iowa, 26 May 1983.

**A-3 The Zimmermans.** Jacob Zimmerman (b. Germany) married Catherine Zaph

- Children: **Jacob Zimmerman jr. (1812 – 1893)** only proven child.

**Jacob Zimmerman Jr. (1812 -1893) married in 1847 Catherine (Rector) Flint (1816 – 1908).** This was the second marriage for both of them.

Jacob's first wife's name is unknown, but their Children were:

- Caroline,
- Jacob III,
- John,
- George,
- Mary.

Catherine's first marriage was to Robert Flint, and their children were:

- Byron (died in infancy),
- Harriet Eliza,
- Albert R.,

- Austin L.,
- Eugene.

Children of **Jacob Zimmerman Jr. (1812 -1893) and Catherine (Rector) Flint (1816 – 1908).**

- **Chauncey W. Zimmerman (1851 – 1929)**
- Nicholas Edgar (b. 1853)

**Chauncey W. Zimmerman (1851 – 1929)** married Jerusha Adelle Eddy (1853 – 1911) in 1873. Their family is detailed in Chapter 1, Section 2.

## Reference:

1. Horton, A. J., The Descendants of Adam Rector; Carl J. Ward Printing, Buffalo, NY, 1915, pages 11 & 12 (Ref. 12).
2. Bolt, Benjamin Darius, To My Children; unpublished working papers for his children documentation of his 1920 – 1950 family research (Ref. 14).
3. Bolt, Ronald Ben & Martin, Nina Leona (Bolt), Bolt Americana (Hayward, California, Ronald Ben Bolt, Copyright 1968.
4. Irish, Mrs. Willis L., A compilation of Jerusha Irish descendants, with Families of Harriet E. Nichols (b. 20 Mar 1831, d. 1 May 1887) and Samuel Eddy (b. 20 April 1829, d. Jan 1890).

**A-4 The Eddys.** William Eddye (original spelling of the family name) was educated at Cambridge, St. Johns and Trinity Colleges, then became a priest in the Episcopal Church of England. In August 1591 he became Vicar of St. Dunstan's Church in Cranbrook, Kent, England, and continued in this assignment until his death in 1616. St. Dunstan's Church has a beautifully illuminated book, written by William Eddye. Ronald Ben Bolt & Nina Leona (Bolt) Martin, authors of Bolt Americana, visited the Church and saw the Vicar's book. William Eddye (b. 1550 – d. 1616) married first Mary Fosten (d. Cranbrook, Kent, England in 1611). Children of William & Mary:

- Mary,
- Phineas,

- Ellen,
- Abigail,
- Anna,
- Elizabeth,
- John (b. 1596),
- **Samuel Eddy (1608 – 1688),**
- Zechariah (b. about 1609),
- Nathaniel (b. about 1610)

Child of William Eddye and his second wife, Sarah Taylor, was Priscilla

**Samuel Eddy (1608 – 1688),** along with his brother, John, came to America in the ship Handmaid, reaching Plymouth 29 October 1630. (See Winthrop's History of New England for an account of this voyage) The brothers apparently dropped the "e" from their surname, and were known by Eddy in America. Samuel Eddy and Elizabeth (Surname unknown) married (date/ place unproven) and lived first in Plymouth. He and others, bought land from the Indians and started the town of Middleborough, Mass. The Indians destroyed the town, but the settlers rebuilt it. The family later moved to Swansea, where he died in 1688. Children of Samuel & Elizabeth Eddy:

- John,
- Caleb,
- Obadiah,
- Hannah,
- **Zechariah (1639 – 1718)**

**Zechariah (1639 – 1718)** married Alice Paddock of Dartmouth and lived in Plymouth, Middleborough, and Swansea, Massachusetts. Children of Samuel & Alice Eddy:

- John,
- Eliza,
- Samuel,
- Ebenezer,
- Caleb,
- Joshua,

- Obadiah,
- **Zechariah Jr. (b. 1664)**

**Zechariah Eddy Jr. (b. 1664)** married first Marcy Baker (date/place not proven) and second Ann Phillis, of Providence, RI. Children of Zechariah Jr. are:

- Alice,
- Elinor,
- Jemima,
- Alice,
- Anne,
- Elisha,
- Joseph,
- Samuel,
- **Zechariah III (b. 1691).**

Marcy Baker was the mother of at least four of his children, but it is not known which children were Marcy's and which were Ann's.

**Zechariah Eddy III (b. 1691)** married Eunice (her surname and their marriage date and place not proven). They lived in Swansea, Massachusetts and Providence & Gloucester, Rhode Island. There is little information concerning this generation, probably due to the revolutionary war. Children of Zechariah Eddy & Eunice:

- Eliphalet,
- **Samuel**,
- Joshua,
- Joseph,
- William,
- Patience,
- Zechariah,
- Benjamin.

**Samuel Eddy** married Deborah Lewis (date/place not proven). Children of Samuel and Deborah (Eddy) Lewis:

- Abigail,
- Lewis,
- **Samuel Jr. (1736 – 1804)**

**Samuel Eddy Jr. (1736 – 1804)** married Margaret (Peggy) Macdonald (date/place unproven). Children of Samuel Jr. and Margaret Eddy:

- Deborah,
- Lewis,
- Barack,
- John,
- Alice,
- Samuel,
- Peggy,
- Levina,
- Asel,
- Patience,
- Anna,
- **Esek (1762 – 1845)**

**Esek Eddy (1762 – 1845)** married Annie Cutler (date/place not proven) and moved to Boston, Erie County, New York. Children of Esek and Annie Eddy:

- Samuel,
- Willard,
- Lewis,
- Susan,
- Erastus,
- **Osmer (1794 – 1849)**

**Osmer Eddy (1794 – 1849)** married (1) Hannah Peck (but their children are not in our line of ancestors. Osmer married (2) 18 May 1828 Phebe Blanchard (1808 - 1868). Children of Osmer and Phebe Eddy:

- **Samuel (1829 – 1890).**
- Andrew Jackson (b. 1830),
- Osmer Jr. (1833 - 1856),
- Amaziah (1836 – 1865),
- Almira (1838 – 1900),
- John (b. 1841),
- James Nelson (b. 1946).

**Samuel Eddy (1829 – 1890)** married in 1850 Harriet Nichols (1831 – 1887) Children of Samuel and Harriet Eddy:

- **Jerusha Adelle (1853 – 1911),**
- Harriet E. (1864 – 1949).

**Jerusha Adelle Eddy married Chauncey W. Zimmerman, and their family is detailed in** Chapter 1, Section 2.

## REFERENCES:

- Bolt, Ronald Ben & Martin, Nina Leona; BOLT AMERICANA
- Eddy, Osmer (1794 – 1849), Family Bible with Family Data (1794 – 1900) Pages of his Eddy Family Births, Marriages and Deaths.
- Bolt, Benjamin Darius, Unpublished working papers on the Descendants of William Eddye, vicar of St. Dunston's Church in Cranbrook, Kent, England.
- Horton, A. J., The Descendants of Adam Rector, Buffalo, NY, 1915
- Irish, Mrs. Willis L., A compilation of Jerusha Irish descendants.

**A-5 The Brubakers.** Jacob Brubaker (b. 1780, d.1836) married Hannah Peters. Their only proven son, Abraham Brubaker (b. 1811, d. 1905) married Martha Ann Parker. Her parents are not proven. She was born 17 August 1815 (possibly in Pennsylvania), and died 8 August 1902. She is buried at Hedley, Nebraska. Their Children:

- Stephen
- Saul

- Solomon
- Henry Isaac
- David
- Molly
- Jennie
- Mary
- Ella
- Jacob
- **Alvah Humbert Brubaker (b. 16 October 1846, d. 24 May 1949) married Anna Marie Hill** - See Chapter 1 Section 3.

References:

1. Kindig, Lucille (Brubaker), Brubaker Family History Letter 1979 (Ref. 57).
2. Brubaker Families in America, Email from E. Renkin to Leland Emet Bolt 5 September 2018. (Ref. 204). Corrects Ref. a names, birth and death dates of Alvah Humbert Brubaker's parents and grandparents.

**A-6 The Hills.** Nathan Hill married Judith (surname, and date/location not proven). Their children:

- Christopher,
- John,
- Thomas,
- Henry,
- Jake,
- Reuben,
- **Anna Maria (1853 – 1944).**

**Anna Maria Hill** Married Alvah Humbert Brubaker **in 1868 at Dixon, IL. (see Chapter 1, Section 3.)**

**A-7 The Fultons.** John Fulton was a native of New York. He was a farmer and became a pioneer. He married Sally Greene (b. New York). Shortly after marriage they moved to Ohio, then to Ogle County, Illinois, where they lived long and useful lives. He died in February 1887, and Sally died three months later. Their children included:

- **George Reynolds Fulton (1839 – 1922).** See Chapter 1, section 4.

## References:

1. Foster, Emma E., History of Marshall County, Kansas; Its People, Industries and Institutions; B. F. Brown & Co., Indianapolis, Indiana 1917 (Ref. 20).
2. Chapman Bros., Chicago, Portrait & Biographical Album, Marshall County, Kansas 1889 (Ref. 137).

**A-8 The Woodcocks.** John Woodcock (b. London, Middlesex, England ABT 1615) immigrated to the American Colonies and married Sarah Curtis in 1644 in Rehoboth, Bristol, Massachusetts. Sarah (b. ABT 1631 in Massachusetts d. 29 November 1676 at Rehoboth, Bristol, Massachusetts). Their children:

- **John Jr.,**
- William,
- Thomas.

**John Woodcock Jr.** (b. ABT 1649 in Roxbury, Suffolk, Massachusetts d. 10 July 1718 at Dedham, Norfolk, Massachusetts) married (1) Sarah Smith 21 February 1673 in Rehoboth, Bristol, Massachusetts. Sarah (b. ABT 1653 in Massachusetts, d. 16 May 1676 Dedham, Norfolk, Massachusetts). They had children:

- **Jeremiah,**
- Nathaniel,
- John

**John Woodcock Jr.** married (2) Sarah Westbrook 5 November 1682 Dedham, Suffolk, Massachusetts. Sarah Westbrook was born 24 July 1651, Norfolk, Massachusetts. Children of John and Sarah (Westbrook):

- John (b. 15 Mar 1684 Dedham, Suffolk, Massachusetts);
- Samuel (b. 18 Nov 1690 Dedham, Suffolk, Massachusetts);
- Sarah (b. ABT 12 Aug 1693 Dedham, Suffolk, Massachusetts);
- Mary (b. ABT 1696 Dedham, Suffolk, Massachusetts).

**Jeremiah Woodcock** (b. 6 January 1765 Rehoboth, Bristol, Massachusetts d. 27 Sep 1752 Needham, Suffolk, Massachusetts) married Mary Metcalf 5 Jan 1698 Dedham, Suffolk, Massachusetts. Mary (b. 3 Oct. 1676 Dedham, Suffolk, Massachusetts). Their children:

- Jeremiah (b. 17 Oct. 1699 Dedham, Suffolk, Massachusetts)
- Margaret (b. 10 Sep 1701 Dedham, Suffolk, Massachusetts);
- Mary (b. 19 Jan 1703 Dedham, Suffolk, Massachusetts);
- **Nathaniel** (b. 14 Sep 1707 Dedham, Suffolk, Massachusetts)
- Barnabas (b. 25 Sep 1709 Dedham, Suffolk, Massachusetts);
- Sarah (b. 1710 Dedham, Suffolk, Massachusetts);
- Michael (b. 1 Dec 1711 Dedham, Suffolk, Massachusetts);
- Miriam (b. ABT 1712 Dedham, Suffolk, Massachusetts).

**Nathaniel Woodcock** (b. 1 December 1707 Dedham, Suffolk, Massachusetts d. 19 October 1750 Stoughton, Suffolk, Massachusetts) married Hannah Barber 27 Nov. 1729 Needham, Bristol, Massachusetts. Hannah (b. 5 Mar 1704 Dedham, Suffolk, Massachusetts). Their Children:

- Samuel (b. 14 Apr. 1731, Stoughton, Norfolk, Massachusetts)
- Margaret (b. 15 Sep 1735, Stoughton, Norfolk, Massachusetts);
- Nehemiah (b. 10 May 1738, Stoughton, Norfolk, Massachusetts);
- Nathaniel (b. 29 Nov 1740, Stoughton, Norfolk, Massachusetts);
- **Nathan** (b. 20 Apr 1743, Stoughton, Norfolk, Massachusetts);
- John (b. ABT 1745, Stoughton, Norfolk, Massachusetts).

**Nathan Woodcock** (b. 20 Apr 1743, Stoughton, Norfolk, Massachusetts d. 14 Aug 1840 Phillipstown, Massachusetts) married Elizabeth Stone Sep

28, 1765 Bridgewater, Plymouth Massachusetts. Elizabeth (b. ABT 1745 in Massachusetts). Their children:

- Nathan Jr. (b. 22 Jun 1766 Easton, Bristol, Massachusetts),
- Elijah (b. 5 June 1768 Easton, Bristol, Massachusetts),
- **Bela** (b. 16 Mar. 1770 Easton, Bristol, Massachusetts),
- Hannah (b. 15 Sep 1772 Easton, Bristol, Massachusetts),
- John (b. 14 Oct. 1775 Easton, Bristol, Massachusetts),
- Daniel (b. 20 Sep1776 Easton, Bristol, Massachusetts),
- Elizabeth (b. 22 Nov 1784 Easton, Bristol, Massachusetts),
- a daughter, Asa, (b. 20 Sep 1789, Bristol, Massachusetts).

**Bela Woodcock** (b. 1770 in Easton, Bristol, Massachusetts d. 14 Aug 1848 Phillipstown, Massachusetts) married Sally Maybury Aug 25, 1791 Norton, Bristol, Massachusetts. Sally (b. 21 May 1770 Easton, Bristol, Massachusetts). Their children:

- Tisdale (b. 15 May 1796 Rutland, Massachusetts);
- Malinda (b. 13 may 1796, Rutland, Massachusetts);
- **Sanford** (b. 21 Nov. 1797, Rutland, Massachusetts);
- Lorinda (b. 27 Nov. 1800, Rutland, Massachusetts);
- Bella Jr. (b. 1 Oct. 1801, Rutland, Massachusetts);
- Alonzo (b. 25 Jul 1803, Rutland, Massachusetts);
- Isaac (b. 10 Oct 1805, Rutland, Massachusetts);
- William W. (b. 29 Sep 1808 Barre. Massachusetts).

**Sanford Maybury Woodcock** (b. 21 Nov. 1797 Rutland, Massachusetts d. 2 December 1877 Worcester, Massachusetts) married Susan Black 9 February 1823 at Leicester, Worcester, Massachusetts. Susan (b. May 1803 Pekham, Massachusetts). Their children:
- Francis (b. 12 Apr 1823),
- Elizabeth Susan (b. 22 Dec1824),
- Jane (b. 14 Aug. 1826),
- Mary (b. 23 Feb 1829),
- Harriet Newhall (b. 8 Oct. 1832),
- Helen Maria (b. 8 Oct 1832 twin of Harriet),

- George (b. 1 Nov 1834),
- **Eliza Ann (b. 28 March 1840, d. 24October 1917),**
- Elmira (b. 17 Feb 1842).

**Eliza Ann Woodcock** married George Reynolds Fulton - See Chapter 1, Section 4.

References:

1. Woodcock Ancestry Search On Line 24 Oct. 2016 Web Site https://familysearch.org/family-tree

2. Federal Census 1880, Marshall County, Kansas, page 81, George Fulton Family.

3. Newspaper, Marysville, Kansas, Advocate Democrat 1 November 1917; Death of Mrs. George Reynolds Fulton.

4. Fulton, Gladys C., Genealogy Letter to Fern Bolt 10 March 1969 (Ref. 49)